Ali Elfadli

Corporate Governance of Banks in Libya

De Gruyter Studies in Corporate Governance

Series editor
Jill Atkins

Volume 1

Ali Elfadli

Corporate Governance of Banks in Libya

DE GRUYTER

ISBN 978-3-11-060074-2
E-ISBN (PDF) 978-3-11-060211-1
E-ISBN (EPUB) 978-3-11-059965-7
ISSN 2570-1673

Library of Congress Control Number: 2019945631

Bibliographic information published by the Deutsche Nationalbibliothek
The Deutsche Nationalbibliothek lists this publication in the Deutsche Nationalbibliografie; detailed bibliographic data are available on the Internet at http://dnb.dnb.de

Typesetting: Integra Software Services Pvt. Ltd.
Printing and Binding: CPI books GmbH, Leck

www.degruyter.com

Contents

1 Introduction

Sound corporate governance is essential within the business environment. Weak corporate governance has led to the failure of many companies around the world, with the result that it has become a growing matter of concern at the global level. One of the most important principles of corporate governance is disclosure (Hawkamah and IFC 2008, OECD 2004); along with other practice, it plays a vital role in ensuring accountability between shareholders, directors and managers. Hawkamah and IFC (2008) argue that a lack of disclosure makes it difficult for shareholders and other stakeholders to monitor the board of directors and managers. This is echoed in the OECD Principles (2004), which assert that the better the quality of disclosure, the less chance there is of corruption in a company or sector. UNCTAD (2011) also sees corporate governance disclosure as playing an important role in ensuring markets function properly.

However, whilst international corporate governance codes acknowledge the importance of disclosure and practice, they tend to ignore the impact that the domestic environment has on these principles. This is problematic, given that developing countries vary from developed countries, and indeed from each other, in terms of their institutional environment. Researchers have responded in recent decades by investigating the role the institutional environment plays in shaping corporate governance disclosure and practice (Grecco, FM Filho, Segura, Sanchez, and Dominguez 2013; Khadaroo and Shaikh 2007; Oliveira, Ceglia, Lima and Ponte 2014). This research monograph seeks to contribute to the ongoing discussion by focusing on corporate governance disclosure in the Libyan banking sector, where the institutional context differs from that in both other developing and developed countries.

The banking sector was chosen as its corporate governance arrangements are set out in law (Lundgren and Catasús 2000) and it is subject to close scrutiny by a range of stakeholders. The sector plays a significant role in the Libyan economy; not only does it account for 50% of all companies listed on the Libyan Stock Market (LSM), but it provides assistance to companies in other sectors by advancing them loans (CBL 2009). Significant reforms have been implemented in the sector over the last decade or so, including the development of a privatization policy and the issuing of first a voluntary (in 2006) and then mandatory (in 2010) corporate governance code by the Central Bank of Libya (CBL). However, despite these reforms and the dramatic changes that have taken place in Libyan culture since the 2011 Arab Spring, very little research has been conducted into corporate governance in this or any other sector in Libya (Larbsh 2010; Magrus 2012; Zagoub 2011). The few studies that have emerged indicate that corporate governance in Libya is still in its infancy. To the best of the author's knowledge, no research has been conducted specifically into corporate governance disclosure within the banking sector. This is, therefore,

https://doi.org/10.1515/9783110602111-001

the focus of this research monograph. The book considers how Libyan commercial banks (LCBs) are responding to national and international corporate governance disclosure requirements.

Understanding how corporate governance operates in emerging societies is crucial to understanding the underlying causes of financial turmoil in these societies (Mitton 2002). As one of the Middle East and North Africa (MENA) countries, Libya shares a number of cultural characteristics (e.g. language, religion and attitudes towards kinship) with its MENA neighbours that distinguish it from developed countries, and affect its approach to corporate governance. At the same time, it differs from its neighbours in that this approach has also been shaped by 42 years of the Gaddafi regime, and by great mineral wealth (Libya produces 1.8 million barrels of oil per day). It is both interesting and useful to understand how corporate governance operates in such a country, which has undergone so much change in recent years. Although clearly the political upheaval in Libya affects all aspects of people's lives as well as the ability of businesses to function, the role of corporate governance in assuaging difficulties and in improving the redevelopment of businesses is crucial and requires research in order to assess its effectiveness in enhancing the business environment as well as ultimately leading to societal improvements.

There is a need to improve corporate governance, especially those aspects related to disclosure, in banks in developing countries. Enhanced disclosure enhances transparency and transparency is a cornerstone of effective governance and accountability (Solomon 2013). This need is particularly urgent in Libya's case as the government has initiated a series of reforms designed to encourage private investment by domestic and foreign shareholders, including the establishment of the LSM in 2006 and the privatization of numerous state-owned enterprises. The dramatic cultural changes that have taken place in some MENA countries, including Libya, as a result of the Arab Spring, also render this research monograph important. Even before the crisis, MENA countries suffered from poor access to finance and a lack of foreign direct investment, and since January 2011, foreign direct investment and market confidence have shown further decline. More than ever, as they embark upon the post-conflict process of transition, these countries need help with corporate governance (IFC 2015). This is especially true in Libya which, unlike its neighbours, Egypt and Tunisia, has seen the Arab Spring revolution give way to war, and national division has fractured its institutions.

There are very few studies investigating corporate governance disclosure and practice in MENA countries, especially in the banking sector, even though this sector has unique characteristics and plays a significant role in the economy of all MENA countries. In Libya, Larbsh (2010) investigated corporate governance practice in Libya from a stakeholder perspective but did not focus on any one industry or corporate governance code. Magrus (2012) examined corporate governance practice in Libyan listed companies following the introduction of the LSM's 2007 code, while Zagoub (2011) investigated how institutional pressures (as evidenced in a tendency towards isomorphism) impact on corporate governance practice in LCBs. However, even since these studies were undertaken, Libyan culture has undergone further fundamental change and more reforms have been implemented in the banking sector, including the introduction of the mandatory corporate governance code (CGLBS2010).

This book contributes to our knowledge by narrowing the literature gap regarding corporate governance disclosure and practice in banking sectors in MENA countries. As mentioned earlier, there is a paucity of research in this area (Darmadi 2013; Feldioreanu and Seriaa 2015; Nwakama, Okereke and Arewa 2011; Thomas and Boolaky 2009; Union of Arab Banks 2007); in Libya's case, there has been no study of corporate governance disclosure and practice in the banking sector since the banking reforms and the significant change in Libyan culture. This research monograph provides information regarding the development of corporate governance disclosure and practice in LCBs since these changes. It gives insights into the level of corporate governance disclosure being offered by Libyan banks, thereby allowing comparison with corporate governance disclosure levels in other developing and developed countries.

The book thus enriches our knowledge by providing evidence of the advances that have been made in the sector in regard to corporate governance disclosure over recent years and by giving an insight into how LCBs are responding to the reforms.

This research monograph sheds light on issues that have been neglected by previous corporate governance disclosure and practice studies, such as the impact of the political and social context on this disclosure and practice. Thus, the research opens a door to further research into corporate governance disclosure and practice in Libya as well as in other MENA countries. This book addresses a gap in the academic literature by investigating corporate governance from a context whose institutional environment differs in key ways from those in both developed and other developing countries.

Lastly, the book provides policy implications for those regulators and policy makers in Libya who are concerned with corporate governance in LCBs. It suggests steps policy makers can take to improve practice not just in the banking sector but across Libya's business environment as a whole.

The book is divided into six chapters. Chapter 2 discusses corporate governance in general terms, including its importance in the banking sector, before focussing specifically on the disclosure requirements. It reviews the existing literature pertaining to corporate governance disclosure and practice in the banking sectors of MENA countries generally and then in Libya.

Chapter 3 presents an overview of the Libyan environment, including the political, economic, religious and cultural context. This context is important as it provides the framework within which the observations of this study should be interpreted and understood. The chapter discusses Libya's uniqueness among its

Arab Spring neighbours before describing the development and current structure of the LBS and proffers a critical review of corporate governance initiatives undertaken so far. The discussion seeks to provide a holistic picture of how the corporate governance principles, including those governing disclosure and transparency, are accommodated within Libya's current legislative/regulatory framework, including any points of difference between Libya's various corporate governance codes and between Libya's framework and those in developed countries.

Chapter 4 presents the theoretical framework of corporate governance. The chapter discusses the traditional theoretical approaches to corporate governance and disclosure before focusing on institutional theory, a theoretical framework that seems to fit the institutional environment under study as well as providing a novel perspective to corporate governance in a MENA economy. The chapter introduces the main institutions that may have an impact on corporate governance disclosure and practice: the bureaucratic state, religion, kinship, the market, politics and the law.

Chapter 5 presents an empirical study of corporate governance disclosure of LCBs and presents the findings from the analysis of LCBs' annual reports and websites. Drawing on each bank's most recent available annual report and/or website (at the time the research was conducted), the empirical research provides a descriptive analysis of corporate governance disclosure performance across the sample as a whole and identifies the level of disclosure in each of the information categories in the ISAR benchmark. Thus, the findings offer an initial overview of recent practice in Libyan commercial banks and the factors that may be shaping this practice. The chapter then compares the disclosure performance of LCBs with that of companies in other developing countries, before analysing the individual disclosure performance of eleven of the sixteen banks, as revealed in websites and annual reports disclosed over the last ten years.

Chapter 6 discusses the findings in the context of the existing literature, concluding that the results are broadly in line with those of other corporate governance studies conducted in developing countries and suggesting that these results provide the most up-to-date picture we have of recent improvements in corporate governance disclosure in Libya. The chapter summarizes the findings of the study and highlights the ways in which the research contributes to existing knowledge. The chapter considers the theoretical and practical implications of the findings before discussing the limitations of the research and offering suggestions for future study.

2 Corporate Governance Disclosure

2.1 Introduction

This chapter provides a review of the literature on corporate governance relevant to the current study. The review focuses on six main areas: defining corporate governance and exploring its importance (and the importance of disclosure and transparency) in the banking sector; reviewing the empirical literature relating to the development of corporate governance in the banking sectors of developed, developing and MENA countries.

The chapter is organized as follows. Section 2.2 discusses the various ways in which corporate governance has been defined and considers its importance. Section 2.3 then focuses on its importance specifically within the banking sector. Section 2.4 reviews the empirical literature relating to the emergence of corporate governance in developed countries (the UK and the US), while Section 2.5 discusses its emergence in developing countries. corporate governance disclosure and transparency requirements are presented in Section 2.6, and the importance of corporate governance disclosure and transparency is discussed in Section 2.7. Section 2.8 reviews the empirical literature relating to corporate governance disclosure in the banking sector, while Section 2.9 reviews the literature focusing specifically on MENA countries and Section 2.10 examines the few studies that address corporate governance disclosure and practice in Libya. Section 2.11 offers a brief concluding discussion.

2.2 Definitions of Corporate Governance

Corporate governance has been defined in several different ways. These definitions can be either narrow or broad in focus, depending on the viewpoint of the policy maker, practitioner, researcher or theorist concerned (Solomon 2013). Those taking a narrower view see corporate governance as simply a mechanism to ensure that management acts to maximize the wealth of ae company's shareholders. Thus Keasey, Thompson and Wright (1997) assert: "In its narrowest sense, the term may describe the formal system of accountability of senior management to the shareholder." (Keasey, Thompson and Wright 1997, p. 2) Shleifer and Vishny (1997) define corporate governance as the "ways in which suppliers of finance to corporations assure themselves of getting a return on their investment" (Shleifer and Vishny 1997, p. 737).

However, critics of this narrow view argue that corporations are not just accountable and responsible to shareholders but to all stakeholders. The Organisation for Economic Co-operation and Development (OECD) states that:

https://doi.org/10.1515/9783110602111-002

> Corporate governance involves a set of relationships between a company's management, its board, its shareholders and other stakeholders. Corporate governance also provides the structure through which the objectives of the company are set, and the means of attaining those objectives and monitoring performance are determined. (OECD 2004, p. 11)

Monks and Minow (2008) define corporate governance as: "the relationship among various participants in determining the direction and performance of corporations" (Monks and Minow 2008, p. 9). Solomon (2013) argues that under the broadest definition, companies are considered accountable to the whole of society, future generations and the natural world. Thus, she defines corporate governance as "the system of checks and balances, both internal and external to companies, which ensures that companies discharge their accountability to all their stakeholders and act in a socially responsible way in all areas of their business activity" (Solomon 2013, p. 17).

Broadening the perspective even further, institutional research has taken a more holistic view of corporate governance, seeing it as a configuration of interdependent elements (Beatty and Zajac 1994) from within and outside the company. As Fiss (2008) explains: "Corporate governance systems themselves are embedded in larger institutional and legal frameworks, and [...] effective practices are highly contingent on the institutional environment in which corporations and their stakeholders are embedded." (Fiss 2008, p. 390) Similarly, Williamson (2000) recognizes that corporate governance is embedded in wider society, while North (1990) argues that corporate governance can be seen as an institutional matrix that determines both the roles played by key actors and the corporation's goals.

2.3 The Importance of Corporate Governance in the Banking Sector

The nature of the banking sector can make corporate governance more problematic than in other sectors. Firstly, the information asymmetry between insider and outsider stakeholders is greater in banks than in other organisations. This can make banks seem more opaque and lead to agency problems; equity and debt holders may find it difficult to control managers who may be more concerned with furthering their own interests than with increasing value, while bidders are unlikely to exert enough control to develop governance significantly. Secondly, the strict regulation to which banks are subject can itself adversely affect corporate governance practice; reassured by the presence of this regulation, stakeholders may make monitoring the bank less of a priority, leaving the way open for managers to take risks. Finally, unlike the industrial sector, the banking sector's monopolistic nature means there is less competition, which also negatively impacts on corporate governance. State ownership in particular significantly shifts the balance of power when it comes to corporate governance (Caprio and Levine 2002).

Addressing these challenges is crucial because effective corporate governance is essential in banks, especially in developing countries, where financial markets tend to be undeveloped. In these countries, banks are usually corporations' main source of finance. They are also the major depositories for government funds, being generally state-owned (La Porta, Lopez-de-Silanes, Shleifer and Vishny 2000). In a government-owned bank, the potential for conflict between depositors and managers increases or decreases according to the credibility of the government, since it is the government that ultimately guarantees deposits; a credible government and political stability will reduce the likelihood of such clashes. Corporate governance problems in these banks arise mainly when the interests of managers conflict with those of the government (Arun and Turner 2004).

In recent years, many developing countries have begun liberalizing their banking sector, privatizing banks and reducing economic regulation. Whilst this has given managers greater freedom in how they run their banks (Arun and Turner 2004), it has also raised problems. The high incidence of domination by family owners, for example, opens the door to the abuse of power by insiders at the expense of outsiders. More generally, both public and private banks in developing countries tend to be less transparent and informative than their counterparts in developed economies (Caprio and Levine 2002). They also tend to lack deposit insurance schemes (Caprio and Levine 2002; Levine 2004). There are thus compelling reasons for focusing on corporate governance in this crucial sector.

2.4 The Development of Corporate Governance in Developed Countries

Concerns about corporate governance in developed countries were widespread towards the end of the 20th century, following widespread corporate failures and a whole array of other corporate scandals that in part led to the publication of the original code of corporate governance best practice, the Cadbury Code in 1992 (Solomon, 2013). The beginning of the 21st century saw little improvement with corporate governance failures attracting significant attention in 2001 with the collapse of Enron, one of America's largest companies. The ensuing scandal focused international attention on the role of corporate governance in preventing company failure. The UK and US responded by strengthening their corporate governance frameworks, with the UK issuing the Combined Code of Corporate Governance in 2003 and the US promulgating the Sarbanes-Oxley Act in 2002. The next sections discuss the historical development of corporate governance in these two countries.

2.4.1 Development of Corporate Governance in the UK

The development of corporate governance in the UK has historically been driven primarily by high profile financial failures (Mallin 2007), starting with the South Sea Bubble in 1720, which prompted the government of the day to introduce reforms designed to protect investors (Dragomir 2008). More than two centuries later, in the early 1990s, several high profile collapses led many to question the reliability of financial reporting and the audit function in the UK (Dulewicz 2004). In an effort to restore investors' confidence in the system, a series of major corporate governance reforms were implemented (Arcot and Brun 2006), the first of these being the issuing of the Cadbury Report in 1992. This gave significant attention to financial reporting and accountability, identifying three main mechanisms of corporate governance: the board of directors, shareholders and auditors (Solomon 2013). The Cadbury Report was followed in 1995 by the Greenbury Report, which aimed to respond to shareholders' concerns about director remuneration and board structure (Mallin 2007). In 1998, the Hampel Report was issued, reviewing the extent to which the recommendations of the Cadbury and Greenbury committees had been implemented. This was followed in 2003 by the Combined Code (Dragomir 2008), which drew together elements from the Cadbury, Greenbury and Hampel reports, along with recommendations issued by the London Stock Exchange (Keasey, Thompson and Wright 2005).

2.4.2 Development of Corporate Governance in the US

The concept of corporate governance emerged in the US between 1929 and 1933 in the wake of the notorious stock market collapse. This collapse was the result of market manipulation, internal trafficking, mismanagement and companies' reckless violation of the rights of shareholders. In response, the US government issued the Securities Act 1933 and the Securities and Exchange Act 1934 (Clarke 2004). Despite these measures, 2001 saw several companies and banks collapse in the US, including Enron and WorldCom and the smaller Tyco and Adelphia (Holmstrom and Kaplan 2003). These failures led to further significant reforms in US corporate governance and the tightening of regulation to protect shareholders. The reforms included the Sarbanes-Oxley Act (2002), which is widely considered to be the most comprehensive reform of US corporate law since the 1930s (Litvak 2007; Solomon 2013).

2.5 The Development of Corporate Governance in Developing Countries

Concerns about corporate governance in developing countries emerged in the late 1990s when it became apparent that poor corporate governance in countries such as Malaysia, South Korea, Singapore, Indonesia, Taiwan and India had been a major cause of the Asian financial crisis (Kim 1998). Researchers turning their attention to developing markets concluded that corporate governance has an essential role to play in these markets, as it has the potential to improve them by facilitating companies' access to finance, reducing the cost of capital and enhancing company performance (Claessens and Yurtoglu 2013). Governance frameworks in developing countries such as Korea have traditionally been insider-dominated and characterized by a lack of separation between ownership and control (Kim 1991), but Solomon, Solomom and Park (2002) noted that in Korea at least, corporate governance systems were starting to become more open to outsiders. These authors also noted the influence the local culture, values and legal framework have on the development of corporate governance. MENA countries share many of the same cultural attributes, and there are broad similarities in terms of regulations and ownership structure. In these countries, the increased focus on corporate governance is a consequence of governmental efforts to develop national markets and attract international investors (CIPE 2003).

2.6 Corporate Governance Disclosure and Transparency Requirements

Disclosure and transparency play an important role in reducing agency problems and information asymmetry between managers and owners (Patel, Balic and Bwakira, 2002). In his definition of disclosure as "[t]he publication by a profit-seeking enterprise of any information relating to its activities with the hope of influencing the judgement and decisions of the users of such information", Wallace (1987, p.133) prioritizes the needs of these owners. Taking a similarly shareholder-oriented view, Abdeen says that "[d]isclosure aims to make sure all material and relevant facts concerning financial position and the results of operations are communicated to users" (Abdeen 1989, p. 51), while Hendriksen defines it as "[t]he presentation of information necessary for the optimum operation of efficient capital markets" (Hendriksen 1982, p. 504). Gibbins, Richardson and Waterhouse describe disclosure as "any deliberate release of financial information, whether numerical or qualitative, required or voluntary, or via formal or informal channels" (Gibbins, Richardson and Waterhouse 1990, p. 122). Cooke also highlights that it can consist of "both voluntary and mandatory items of information" (Cooke 1992, p. 231). These may be "provided in the financial statements, notes to the accounts, management's analysis of operations for the current and forthcoming year and any supplementary information" (Cooke 1992, p. 231).

However, as Hill and Jones explain, companies deal with a whole range of stakeholders, all of whom have reason to be interested in the information it provides:

> Stockholders provide the firm with capital. In exchange, they expect the firm to maximise the risk-adjusted return on their investment. Creditors provide the firm with finance and in exchange expect their loans to be repaid on schedule. Managers and employees provide the firm with time, skills, and human capital commitments. In exchange, they expect fair income and adequate working conditions. Customers supply the firm with revenues and expect value for money in exchange. Suppliers provide the firm with inputs and seek fair prices and dependable buyers in exchange [...] The general public, as tax payers, provide the firm with a national infrastructure. In exchange, they expect corporate citizens who enhance and/or do not damage the quality of life and do not violate the rules of the game established by the public through their legislative agents. (Hill and Jones 1992, p. 133)

All of these stakeholder groups have a direct interest in knowing what the company is doing. Disclosure and transparency is an important corporate governance mechanism (Bushman, Chen, Engel and Smith 2004; Hawkamah and IFC 2008; OECD 2004) because it ensures that officers and directors are held accountable not just to shareholders but to all these stakeholders.

Recognizing the importance of the concept, the OECD Principles (2004) stipulate that "[t]he corporate governance framework should ensure that timely and accurate disclosure is made on all material matters regarding the corporation, including the financial situation, performance, ownership, and governance of the company" (OECD 2004, p. 49). Countries around the world have come to the same conclusion and taken steps to improve their corporate governance disclosure requirements. The US, for example, issued new disclosure rules in 2009 in relation to risk management, while the European Commission has changed a number of its corporate governance disclosure requirements. Developing countries have also strengthened their corporate governance disclosure requirements as they have become more involved in the global economy. Disclosure requirements are a key concern within the OECD Principles (2004), the EU Transparency Directive and the Commonwealth Association for Corporate Governance (CACG) Guidelines, and are a core element of national codes around the world, including South Africa's King II Report on Corporate Governance, the UK's Cadbury Report (1992) and Combined Code (2003), and the US's Sarbanes-Oxley Act (2002). In the MENA countries also, disclosure and transparency have been the focus of numerous corporate governance codes and private sector initiatives. In 2003, a regional initiative was launched by the World Bank's Global Corporate Governance Forum (GCGF), the Center for International Private Enterprise (CIPE) and local partners in Egypt, Jordan, Lebanon and Morocco to assess the state of corporate governance in selected MENA countries (Saidi 2004).

The OECD (2004) asserts that disclosure should include, but not be limited to: material information on the financial and operating results of the company; company objectives; major share ownership and voting rights; remuneration policy for members of the board and key executives; information about board members, including their qualifications, the selection process, other company directorships and whether they are regarded as independent by the board; related party transactions; foreseeable risk factors; and governance structures and policies, especially the content of any corporate governance code or policy and how it is to be implemented. All information should be prepared and disclosed in accordance with international accounting standards and other standards for financial and non-financial disclosure. The OECD's requirements in terms of corporate governance disclosure and transparency are discussed in more detail in Section 3.4.3.

2.7 The Importance of Corporate Governance Disclosure and Transparency

The importance of corporate governance disclosure and transparency has become increasingly evident since the financial crisis, with numerous studies identifying lack of financial disclosure and inadequate supervision of directors as the main causes of the crash. This has led to more demands for regulation and tighter disclosure requirements, while accounting standards have become more complex in an effort to protect markets. There is now a general view that companies must disclose accurate and timely information to shareholders and the public regarding their financial performance, liabilities, ownership and corporate governance (Fung 2014) so that investors (and potential investors) can accurately judge the risk and rewards associated with any investment (OECD 2004). There is a clear relationship between disclosure and corporate governance; information disclosure is both integral to the effective operation of all internal and external governance mechanisms and an indicator of whether these mechanisms are functioning properly (Lu and Chen 2009). It is not surprising then that Beeks and Brown)2006) found a direct positive correlation between the level of disclosure in companies and the quality of governance. Disclosure benefits not just individual investors but also the market at large; having access to good information enables the market to evaluate a company's governance and the extent to which it reacts to shareholder needs. Not only may this uncover potential risk, but it may also give an indication of the direction of future cash flows (UNCTAD 2011).

2.8 The Influence of Culture on Corporate Governance

Hofstede (1980) calls culture "[t]he collective programming of the mind which distinguishes the members of one group or society from those of another" (Hofstede 1980, p. 25). As these learned values and beliefs shape attitudes and behaviours (Hofstede 1984), affecting how individuals communicate within and across social systems, culture plays an important role in forming the norms and values of these systems. Understanding culture is therefore important to understanding changes in the social system (Harrison and McKinnon 1986).

The notion that people and organisations within a system tend to behave in broadly similar ways is consistent with an institutional theory perspective which posits that behaviour is institutionalized by social values and norms (DiMaggio and Powell 1983; Friedland and Alford 1991; Scott 2008). The impact of the institutional environment on corporate governance disclosure and practice has been demonstrated in several studies. Khadaroo and Shaikh (2007) found that institutional isomorphism has an impact on corporate governance practice, while Deephouse (1996) found a link between institutional isomorphism (structures, strategies and practices) and legitimacy in the banking sector. He found that society and regulators are more accepting of banks that conform to common practice than of banks demonstrating atypical behaviour, and that older or larger banks, which tend to exert greater influence and to be more visible, are held to an even higher standard. Investigating the impact of culture on corporate governance in Saudi Arabia, Bukhari (2014) found that while family and kinship networks have had an adverse impact on the emergence and development of corporate governance (e.g. by allowing abuses of authority and conflicts of interest to go unchecked), the bureaucratic state and religion appear to have positively influenced compliance levels. Finally, Madhani (2015), investigating the influence of the national institutional, legal and regulatory environment on firm-level corporate governance mechanisms, compared the governance and disclosure practices of MNC subsidiaries listed in India and domestic cross-listed firms listed in the US/Europe. He found the level of disclosure to be significantly higher in the domestic cross-listed firms than in the MNC subsidiaries, which he attributed to the differences in institutional and legal environment.

2.9 Corporate Governance Disclosure in the Banking Sector

A few studies have examined corporate governance disclosure in the banking sectors of Indonesia, Nigeria, Japan and Canada, assessing the level of disclosure against local and international codes (Nwakama, Okereke and Arewa 2011; Darmadi 2013; Feldioreanu and Seriaa 2015; Maingot and Zeghal 2008; Thomas and Boolaky 2009). All focus specifically on this aspect of corporate governance. All of the studies draw their data from annual reports, apart from Maingot and Zeghal (2008), who utilize annual reports and websites.

Darmadi (2013) found that large and long-established banks disclose more information than small ones, but that the latter tend to disclose more about their board members. The banks in this study disclosed least about their internal controls and external auditing. Darmadi suggests that the generally low level of disclosure may be attributable to a lack of awareness among bank managers, but Maingot and Zeghal (2008) argue that the choice to disclose and the extent of the disclosure are influenced rather by managers' strategic considerations. Their study highlights the importance of the annual report as a source of corporate governance disclosure and concludes that as small banks tend to copy one another's corporate governance disclosure, they tend to publish almost exactly the same information.

In their Japan-based study, Thomas and Boolaky (2009) found that the extent of corporate governance disclosure in the country's banks is influenced by a range of factors including the number of non-executive directors on the board, the level of cross-ownership, the capital adequacy ratio and auditor quality. They identify non-executive directors as having a more significant impact than either the size of the bank's total assets or external audit firms. Feldioreanu and Seriaa (2015), meanwhile, observe that culture also has an impact on the level of corporate governance disclosure. Their study also highlights the tendency of more profitable banks to disclose more information than less profitable institutions, though the size of the bank does not appear to have a major influence.

2.10 Corporate Governance Disclosure in MENA Countries

To date, relatively few studies, indeed only four have focused specifically on corporate governance disclosure among companies in MENA countries. A more general investigation of corporate governance practice in MENA countries was conducted by the Union of Arab Banks (2007), which surveyed 67 banks across Qatar, Oman, the UAE, Yemen, Jordan and Egypt. Although this is not the prime focus, the study does look at the level of disclosure and transparency in Arab banks, finding it to be satisfactory. It observes that there is general compliance with international standards regarding external auditing, the preparation and dissemination of information, the functions of the internal audit, the regulation and rotation of auditors, board access to external auditors' reports and training programmes, the disclosure of transactions, meetings with ratings analysts and employees' remuneration schemes. However, it notes that there are weaknesses in regard to the disclosure of information concerning shareholder rights, credit risk assessment and the implications of clients' corporate governance practices. This general trend seems to also be reflected in Al-Malkawi, Pillai and Bhatti's (2014) findings. Investigating corporate governance practice across several Gulf countries, these authors found that companies in these countries adhere to 69% of the OECD's (2004) recommendations, with firms listed in the United Arab Emirates stock markets exhibiting the highest level of compliance, followed by those in Oman, Saudi Arabia, Qatar and Kuwait.

Samaha, Dahawy, Hussainey and Stapleton (2012) are among the few researchers to focus specifically on corporate governance disclosure in a MENA country – in this case, Egypt. They found that although levels of corporate governance are minimal in Egyptian listed companies, there is a high level of disclosure for items that are mandatory under the Egyptian Accounting Standards (EASs). Socio-economic factors seem to be significant in shaping corporate governance disclosure practice in Egypt; the study found that role duality and higher ownership concentration, as measured by block-holder ownership, are both linked to lower levels of corporate governance disclosure, while the proportion of independent directors on the board and firm size are positively correlated with higher levels of disclosure. The study concludes that Egyptian listed companies disclose corporate governance information in order to reduce information asymmetry and agency costs and to improve investor confidence in the reported accounting information. Al-Moataz and Hussainey (2012), meanwhile, used content analysis to investigate the determinants of corporate governance disclosure in Saudi companies, finding that board independence, audit committee size, profitability, liquidity and gearing are the main determinants. In contrast to Samaha, Dahawy, Hussainey and Stapleton (2012), they found no statistically significant association between firm size and corporate governance disclosure.

In their comparative study, Othman and Zeghal (2010) found that the colonial background of the MENA country has an impact on the level of disclosure and transparency found within its companies. They found that countries having historical links with the UK exhibit substantially higher Transparency and Disclosure T&D scores than those from countries having historical links with France. Companies operating in the information technology sector also exhibit higher levels of transparency and disclosure. Their multivariate analysis revealed that the nature of the business culture, company size and the perceived importance of intangibles all affect the level of transparency and disclosure among companies in the MENA region.

2.11 Corporate Governance Disclosure and Practice in Libya

Larbsh (2010) gave an early insight into corporate governance practice, including disclosure and transparency, in Libya, using a mix of qualitative and quantitative methods to investigate corporate governance from the stakeholder perspective. His study provided a preliminary understanding of corporate governance practice in the Libyan context, including the impact of cultural factors. It presents a picture of an under-developed corporate governance framework and a country that is lagging behind its neighbours. Larbsh argues that the lack of corporate governance principles has led to weak accountability and responsibility processes in Libya: a problem that has been exacerbated by the country's opaque economic structure, outdated legal system, cultural and social norms, political interference and a lack of accounting professionalism. The weakness of the education system and low levels of stakeholder activism are also cited as factors affecting the implementation of the corporate governance framework. Among its suggestions for future research, the study points to the need to investigate the obstacles to disclosure and transparency in Libya.

Magrus (2012) subsequently investigated the nature and extent of corporate governance practice in eight listed Libyan companies following the introduction of the LSM's corporate governance code (CGLSM 2007). Using semi-structured interviews and questionnaires, the study gathered the perceptions of senior managers and employees in finance-related positions, along with those of Libyan academics and auditors. It identified the obstacles blocking the application of the CGLSM and sought the opinions of regulators and officials on how these might be removed. The findings of the study reveal that corporate governance in Libya is still in the early stages of development; it identifies a weak legal environment, lack of knowledge about corporate governance, poor leadership, lack of training among directors and poor awareness among investors. It also highlights the influence of social, cultural and economic factors. The results suggest that urgent action is needed if a robust and effective corporate governance system is to be implemented in Libya. Magrus echoes Larbsh in arguing that further investigation is needed into corporate governance mechanisms, including disclosure and transparency, because of their importance to Libya's economic development.

Turning to the banking sector in particular, Zagoub (2011) found that corporate governance practice and reform in LCBs have primarily been driven by the CBL and banking legislation. Institutional pressures have had more impact on some banks than others, and banks have responded differently to these pressures. Zagoub concludes that the CBL needs to put more pressure on LCBs to improve corporate governance and to offer them greater support. However, Zagoub's study, although useful, has some important limitations. For example, in his suggestions for future research, he acknowledge the urgent need for more research into particular aspects of corporate governance such as disclosure. More importantly, he fails to consider the impact of the CBL's 2010 Corporate Governance Code for Libyan Banks (CGLBS 2010) and how banks are responding strategically to its requirements, or the extent to which this code is relevant to the Libyan banking sector and environment and whether it was issued in response to local or institutional pressures.

Among the studies focusing specifically on disclosure, Ellabbar (2007) investigated the role of accounting disclosure in creating an efficient capital market in Libya. Ellabar drew on the International Accounting Standards (IAS) and the findings of previous studies to develop a disclosure index, with which he was able to conclude that "[t]he average disclosure rate of the top 10 companies is 56% in Libya, and all the Libyan construction companies sampled had a disclosure rate of less than 80%" (Ellabbar 2007, p. 149). The study also found that

> [t]he information published by Libyan companies is insufficient for accurate evaluations and not available to all users on time. Most Libyan companies delay the publication of their financial statements, or if they are published, they are not audited. In addition, there are no channels available for issuing this information, such as financial magazines or newspapers.
>
> (Ellabbar 2007, p. 148)

Osama's (2013) investigation of transparency and disclosure in Libyan companies was comprehensive, encompassing listed and unlisted, and private and publicly owned companies across a range of sectors. He found that although the level of transparency and disclosure had demonstrated a statistically significant increase overall during the review period, it was still low compared to other countries (developed and developing) when judged using Standard and Poor's (S&P) data. He also found significant variations in disclosure levels between different types of company:

> Companies listed in the LSM provided more T&D than those not listed, the public sector provided more T&D than the private sector, the banking sector provided more T&D than the insurance sector and companies with audit peer reviews provided more T&D than those without. Whilst small companies provided more T&D than other companies, the variation in levels of T&D for different age groups was unclear. (Osama 2013, p. 27)

Only two studies have addressed disclosure practice specifically in the Libyan banking sector. The first of these was conducted by Kribat (2009), who assessed the financial disclosure practices of eight banks as revealed in their annual reports. A disclosure index covering both mandatory and voluntary items was constructed to measure the extent of disclosure over the period 2000–2006, the aim being to examine the relationship between certain firm-specific characteristics (such as bank size, the age of the bank, profitability and ownership structure) and the overall level of financial disclosure. The results indicated that none of the banks in the sample had complied fully even with the mandatory disclosure requirements in any of the sample years.

The second study was conducted by Hawashe (2014). This study picked up where Kribat's left off, investigating the level of voluntary disclosure in the Libyan banking sector over the period 2006–2012. Hawashe also sought to establish whether there was any significant association between seven commercial bank-specific attributes (i.e. age of bank, size of bank, bank liquidity position, profitability, government ownership, foreign ownership and listing status) and the extent of voluntary disclosure over the review period. This study employed a disclosure index made up of 63 information items. Hawashe found that although the extent of voluntary disclosure remained low, it had increased gradually during the period of the study.

2.12 Summary

This chapter began by discussing the debate that surrounds how the concept of corporate governance should be defined. It offers examples of narrow and broad definitions of corporate governance before discussing the recent emergence of a more institution-oriented interpretation of the concept. The development of corporate governance in developed and developing countries is briefly outlined, followed by its particular importance within the banking sector. The chapter then moves on to corporate governance disclosure and transparency. This part of the chapter ends by highlighting the central importance of disclosure and transparency within corporate governance and the impact of culture on corporate governance.

Finally, the chapter reviews the literature addressing corporate governance disclosure in the banking sector in developed and developing countries, including those in the MENA region. The review highlights that such studies are relatively rare, and that most of those that are conducted concentrate on developed countries. Those that are conducted in developing countries tend to focus on the practice of corporate governance in general rather than the disclosure mechanism in particular, even though disclosure requirements feature in most local and international corporate governance codes. Where the focus is disclosure, most seek to describe its extent, rather than to establish any link with specific theories such as institutional theory. The book seeks to address this literature gap, and to introduce a fresh theoretical perspective, by considering corporate governance disclosure in one developing country named Libya from the perspective of institutional theory.

The review identifies that there have been few studies investigating corporate governance in the Libyan banking sector, and that none of these addresses disclosure in any depth. This represents an opportunity: to explore the sector in more detail so that it becomes possible firstly, to compare the disclosure performance of LCBs with that of companies in other developing countries and secondly, to assess whether and how this performance has improved in recent years.

3 The Libyan Context

3.1 Introduction

Over recent decades, researchers (e.g. La Porta, Lopez-de-Silanes, Shleifer and Vishny 1997; La Porta, Lopez-de-Silanes, Shleifer and Vishny 1998; La Porta, Lopez-de-Silanes and Shleifer 1999; La Porta, Lopez-de-Silanes, Shleifer and Vishny 2000) have emphasized the need to investigate the nature of corporate governance in emerging economies in order to understand what lies behind their financial instability. Researchers have argued that organisational practice is shaped by the institutional context (Feldman and Rafaeli 2002; Peng 2003), but that this context is often unstable in developing countries as a result of inadequate legal and regulatory frameworks (North 1990; Young Peng, Ahlstrom, Bruton and Jiang 2008). Under pressure from international organisations or internal reforms, some have imported Anglo-Saxon or European systems (Young, Peng, Ahlstrom, Bruton and Jiang 2008), but the influence of informal institutions such as family and kinship ties, business groups and government connections remains pervasive (Jiang and Peng 2011; Peng and Heath 1996). A lack of market institutions such as a product market, takeover market and labour market has also hindered the development of corporate governance in these countries (Groves, Hong, McMillan and Naughton 1995).

Previous studies investigating corporate governance in the Arab context have tended to assume that because they share the key cultural attributes of language and religion, these countries are broadly homogeneous. However, this overlooks the fact that Arab countries have different political systems, are located in different continents and are home to a wide variety of ethnic groups (Abubaker 2007). These differences should be taken into account when considering institutional context. This chapter seeks to give some insight into the institutional context in Libya by giving a broad overview of the country. It briefly describes Libya's main demographic attributes, the development of its political and economic systems, and how it differs from other Arab Spring countries, before discussing the country's banking sector and the legal framework that governs it. The second half of the chapter considers how this legal framework addresses the various aspects of corporate governance, both generally and in the banking sector in particular, and compares it with corporate governance principles in developed countries. This discussion of the institutional environment should equip the reader with a preliminary understanding of the institutional factors shaping corporate governance disclosure and practice in Libya's banking sector.

https://doi.org/10.1515/9783110602111-003

3.2 General Background

Located on Africa's Northern coast, Libya covers a vast area of 1,760,000 square kilometres equal to the combined area of the UK, Germany and France (OBG 2008). One of the MENA countries, Libya's position between Europe, Asia and Africa (see Figure 3.1) has made it economically valuable, and it has benefited for centuries from the trade routes that cross its borders. Much of the southern part of the country falls within the Sahara Desert. Libya has a population of almost six million (last recorded in 2006). The main language is Arabic, and Islam is the country's only religion. Libya became independent in 1952 after a long period of foreign occupation (1911–1951), but in 1969, Colonel Muammar Gaddafi overthrew the king and took control of the government, holding onto power for 42 years (Ahmad and Gao 2004).

3.2.1 Political and Economic Context

Libya's economy did not start to develop until 1959 and the discovery of oil (Bait El-Mal, Smith and Taylor 1973). Between independence in 1952 and the military coup of 1969, the economic system was capitalist, with most commercial enterprises being privately owned. The government implemented a number of measures during this period to strengthen the economy, including enacting import and export legislation to protect local industries and establishing the Industrial and Real Estate Bank of Libya to furnish loans to local entrepreneurs and provide technical and economic services for both public and private sector organisations (Bait El-Mal, Smith and Taylor 1973).

However, with the military coup, things changed significantly. New policies were introduced in 1972, including changes to the administrative and legislative system, and the regime declared itself socialist and intent on devolving power to the people. Gaddafi's new system differed from both capitalism and communism in its rejection of the idea of political parties. Its main principles were set out in The Green Book, written by Gaddafi himself (US Commercial Service 2008). In 1977, the regime announced further important changes, including the declaration of the people's authority and a change of name from the Libyan Arab Republic to the Socialist People's Libyan Arab Jamahiriya. The country's new constitution was based on the Qur'an, and political power was devolved to the people, to be exercised through the People's Congress, people's committees, syndicates, unions and professional associations.

This period saw the nationalization of foreign companies, the establishment of public-owned companies and restrictions placed on private companies. Eventually, most companies in the manufacturing sector, foreign and domestic retail trade and banking and insurance sectors came to be owned and controlled by the state (Kilani 1988). However, once state-owned, many became inefficient, to the detriment of the overall economy. The government responded by starting to relax controls in the private sector and in 1987, it launched its liberalization strategy with the aim of converting the economic system from a planned economy to a market economy. An important step encouraging liberalization was the promulgation of Law No.8/1988 permitting the private ownership of retail businesses and small-scale manufacturing companies. This was followed in 1992 by Law No.2 permitting the sale of state property to non-governmental Libyan interests (US Commercial Service 2008). These laws and policies played an important role in improving the economy and reducing the pressure on the government's general budget resulting from the decline in global oil prices. Another important law was established in 1997; Law No.5/1997 set out the terms upon which foreigners could invest in Libya (US Commercial Service 2008). Finally, 1999 saw the arrival of Act No.9 allowing so-called free zones. This act also played an important role in encouraging privatization (US Commercial Service 2008). Throughout this period, the government's chief policy aim was to engineer the transition from a directed economy to a free market by encouraging foreign investment, the development of the capital market and privatization.

By the end of 2010, the whole MENA region was experiencing dramatic changes which were having (and indeed continue to have) major impacts on these countries' politics, economies and cultures. The revolution that began in Tunisia spread to Egypt, Libya, Syria and Yemen, and the period became known as the Arab Spring. The build up to the Libyan revolution began on 15th February 2011 when protesters attacked security officers in Benghazi, demanding the release from custody of one of their members. The protesters were relatives of 1200 detainees who had been killed by the regime in an alleged prison uprising in 1996. From this initial spark, the protest spread to the city of Albida, east of Benghazi, and it was here that the first protesters were killed by the regime. On 17th February, the protests spread to Benghazi. The regime, seeking to crack down on the demonstrators, killed hundreds in four days, but it quickly lost control not just of the cities in the east but also of western cities such as Misrata, Zawiya, Zuara and Alzentan.

On the 2nd March 2011, an interim parliament, the National Transitional Council (NTC), was founded and an interim government was formed. Many countries around the world were quick to recognize the NTC as the representative authority of Libya. On 19th March, Gaddafi's army attacked Benghazi in an attempt to regain control, only to face armed resistance from the revolutionaries and bombing by NATO warplanes. After the attack, the rest of the international community gradually accepted the NTC as the sole legitimate representative of the Libyan people. On 3rd August 2011, the NTC issued the Libyan Constitutional Declaration as an interim measure pending the completion of a permanent constitution. As a result of this interim constitution, a number of existing laws were consolidated and new laws were issued. The 20th October 2011 saw the killing of Gaddafi by the revolutionaries, bringing to an end a war which had lasted for eight months. Three days later, the NTC announced that Libya had been liberated and that it was now the country's sole representative authority. On 7th July 2012, Libyans were able to vote for the first time in 42 years. Two hundred representatives were elected to form a parliament and charged with the task of managing the transition period, building state institutions and drafting a new constitution. On 20th February 2013, Libyans elected a committee of 60 members to draft a permanent constitution (at the time of writing, Libya is still being governed by the terms of the NTC's interim constitution).

3.2.2 Corruption and Instability

According to the CPI (2010), corruption is a problem in Libya, despite the law against it. The severity of the issue was highlighted in 2009, when Libya was ranked 130th out of 180 countries on Transparency International's corruption perception indicator. Corruption negatively affects all of Libya's business sectors, including banking. Bribery and favouritism are common practice in all sectors, and all businesses, particularly those that are state-owned, struggle with the unfair competition that dominates the local market (GAN 2016). The origins of this corruption may be traced back to the Gaddafi regime, where it flourished unchecked in the absence of democracy, the rule of law and a free press. This was acknowledged even by Gaddafi's own son, Seif al-Islam, who admitted: "*In all frankness and* transparency, there is no freedom of the press in Libya; actually there is no press, even, and there is no real 'direct people's democracy' on the ground." (Committee to Protect Journalists 2007) Corruption worsened during the revolutionary period when the country's institutional framework was weak and the rule of law was impacted by instability and violence (GAN 2016). At the time of writing, judicial institutions in Libya remain corrupted, while political factionalism and powerful militias are hampering the government's efforts at law enforcement.

It was expected that the Libyan Constitution Drafting Assembly would have finished the constitution by late March 2016 (Democracy Reporting International 2016), but as of May 2017, Libya still has no permanent constitution, and the constitutional declaration issued by the NTC in 2011 remains the country's supreme legal code. Libya lacks the comprehensive legal framework it needs to tackle corruption properly, there being no general anti-corruption law. Instead, the authorities must rely on the Libyan Criminal Code and a specialized anti-corruption law. After the revolution, the NTC issued Act No.192/2010, which sets out National Standards of Integrity, but in the absence of an institutional framework capable of enforcing it, the act has made no real impact (GAN 2016).

3.2.3 Religion

Religion has a fundamental impact in Arab countries, including Libya. It plays a main role in Libyan society, shaping the country's culture (Aghila 2000) and influencing individuals' behaviour and relationships, not just in the private sphere but also in business. Consequently, the practice of companies and banks is also impacted by religion (Abouzkeh 2013). All Libyans without exception are Muslims, though the more than one million foreigners living in Libya follow a range of religions including Christianity and Indo-Chinese faiths without facing any constraints (Attir and Al-Azzabi 2004). Since achieving independence, all of Libya's constitutions have positioned Islam as the country's main religion, though the NTC's interim constitutional declaration (2011), while citing Islamic Sharia as the main source for the country's legislation, also guarantees non-Muslims freedom of religious practice. Legislation is informed by the Qur'an and Sunnah, while religion also impacts government policy (OBG 2008).

3.2.4 Kinship and Family

Along with religion and language, the attitudes and behaviours of Libyans are also significantly impacted by family (Pratten and Mashat 2009). The concept of kinship, not just within the extended family but also within the tribe or clan, is the cornerstone of Libyan society and fundamental in shaping not just social but also business life. Individuals are loyal to their kinship ties and their region. Each family, tribe and clan has rules and traditions which have to be respected by members, who can bring honour or dishonour to the name and reputation of the family or clan through their good or bad behaviour (Agnaia 1997). Within the family, the hierarchical order is structured according to age and generation, with the role of head of the family being held by grandfather, father or eldest son (Ritchie and Khorwatt 2007).

Within the business environment, it is often these kinship relationships, rather than qualifications or experience, that determine whether individuals are appointed or promoted (Agnaia 1997). Ritchie and Khorwatt (2007) indicate that this expectation of loyalty poses interesting challenges in terms of the auditors' professional requirement to maintain independence: "Since the client is highly likely to be from the same socio-cultural group, the pressure on the auditor may be to certify financial statements which do not fully comply with the professional standards." (Ritchie and Khorwatt 2007, p. 42) Several studies have explored the impact of family on the development of corporate governance in emerging societies. Bukhari (2014), for example, found that family and kinship institutions appear to have negatively impacted the emergence and development of corporate governance in Saudi Arabia in terms of issues surrounding control, abuse and conflicts of interest, while Filatotchev, Lien and Piesse (2005) found that boards perform better when they are independent of the founding family.

3.2.5 Libya and Arab spring countries

The previous sections discuss a number of cultural characteristics that Libya has in common with its MENA neighbours and that differentiate it from western and developed countries. Despite these cultural similarities, however, the events of the Arab Spring unfolded very differently, and have had very different long-term impacts, in the five MENA countries that experienced them. Libya is one of three states to see a change in leadership, but it is unique in being the only state in which the old regime has not yet been replaced with a new national government. In Tunisia and Egypt, civilian protesters, with the help of the army, were able to force the regime to step down after several days, and the army played a significant role in maintaining security and supervising the transition of power. In Libya, however, it was the killing of protesters by Gaddafi's army (see Section 3.2.1) that changed a civilian uprising into an armed revolution that lasted for eight months and destabilised the whole country. Unlike Tunisia and Egypt, who have successfully made the transition to a new regime and a new constitution, Libya remains unstable; it still has no permanent constitution, and power has been split between factions, one of which controls the east and the other the west of the country.

Economically, Libya has also been harder hit than the other two countries because of its heavy reliance on a single industry – oil and gas production. A member of the Organisation of Petroleum Exporting Countries (OPEC), Libya possesses the largest oil reserves in the African continent, before the civil war exporting nearly 1.8 million barrels of oil per day as well as significant amounts of natural gas. Energy production accounted for 95% of total export earnings within the country, 60% of total GDP, and 80% of government revenue. However, the civil war and its aftermath have disrupted both the production and exportation of oil and gas, causing major damage to the economy. The political and economic turbulence have badly affected the banking sector, with the CBL being divided between Libya's eastern and western governments, and the commercial banks suffering a systemic liquidity crunch (Chami, Al-Darwish, Cevik, Charap, George, Gracia and Pattanayak 2012).

3.3 The Libyan Banking Sector

This section discusses the Libyan banking sector (LBS), including its historical development, structure, legal framework and recent reforms. The sector plays an essential role in Libya's economy by providing financial support to businesses and individuals (Elkington 2004; Moyo and Rohan 2006; Abouzkeh 2013), though as Levine (2004) has observed, banks are "more opaque than nonfinancial firms" and can "readily hide problems by extending loans to clients that cannot service previous debt obligations" (Levine 2004, p. 9). The sector's importance is heightened by the fact that it is the only source of such finance – unlike other MENA countries such as Tunisia and Egypt, the stock market does not play a key role in generating funds for investment (Husien and Havard 1990). Despite its key economic role, however, there are as yet very few studies addressing corporate governance in the LBS.

3.3.1 The History of the Libyan Banking Sector

Libya's first bank was established in 1898, during the Ottoman Empire period. An agricultural bank, it had a branch in each of Libya's two main cities: Tripoli and Benghazi (CBL 2006). The bank ceased trading in 1911 when the occupying Italian government (1911–1943) allowed Italian banks such as Banco De Roma, Banco De Napoli, Banco De Sicilia and the Bank of Italy to open branches in Libya. Italy had several reasons for establishing these banks; not only did it want to play a greater role in the Libyan economy, but it also wanted to provide financial services to Italian immigrants and the military government (CBL 2006). Later, during the military administration by the British and French (1943–1951), Barclays opened two branches in Benghazi and Tripoli, alongside the Italian banks, which continued to operate after the end of the Second World War.

In 1951, the United Nations decided to give Libya its independence. Four new banks were established between 1951 and 1969, including Libya's first domestic bank, the Libyan International Bank, established in 1955. This bank had the authority to issue banknotes and coins as well as to supervise and monitor the activities of commercial banks in Libya. In 1963, Law No.4 changed the name of the bank to the Central Bank of Libya and gave it administrative authority over the entire Libyan banking sector. The law also restricted foreign banks to holding a maximum of 49% of the equity of their operations in Libya; as a result, they were obliged to sell the balance of their holdings to the Libyan private sector (CBL 2006).

As mentioned in Section 3.2.1, in 1969, a military coup brought about a significant change in Libyan politics. Motivated by communist ideology, the new military government implemented a policy of nationalization and began gradually buying up the remaining foreign-owned shares in commercial banks. In this way, Barclays Bank, Banco di Roma, Banco di Napoli and the Arab Bank came to be 100% owned by the Libyan government, which reorganized and renamed them. The newly reorganized sector was made up of the CBL plus four commercial banks, three of which were entirely government-owned (Umma Bank, Jumhoriya Bank and the National Commercial Bank) and one of which (the Sahara Bank) was still 49% owned by private investors. The sector also contained three specialized banks (Abouzkeh 2013; Abdussalam 1985; Abida 2011), all of which were government-owned. By 1977, all banks, including private domestic banks, were state-owned. Table 3.1 summarizes the structure of the sector over the period 1969–1993, including the capital structures of the banks, the dates they were established and type of ownership.

Table 3.1: Structure of the Banking System 1969–1993.

Name of bank	Establishment date	Type of bank	% of shares owned by CBL	% of shares owned by private sector	Former name
Central Bank of Libya	1971	Central	100%	0%	Libyan International Bank
National Commercial Bank	1970	Commercial bank	100%	0%	– Commercial Banking Division of CBL – Istiklal Bank (Bank of Napoli as a foreign bank) – Orouba Bank (a branch of the Arab Bank as a foreign bank)
Umma Bank	1969	Commercial bank	100%	0%	Bank of Rome
Jumhoriya Bank	1969	Commercial bank	100%	0%	Barclays Bank
Sahara Bank	1970	Commercial bank	51%	49%	– Bank of North Africa – Wahda Arabia Bank – African Banking Company – Other small banks
Agricultural Bank	1970	Specialized bank	100%	0%	Libyan National Agricultural Bank
Savings and Real Estate Investment Bank	1981	Specialized bank	100%	0%	– The Industrial and Real Estate Bank of Libya
Development Bank	1972	Specialized bank	100%	0%	

Source: Abida (2011)

3.3.2 Current Structure of the Libyan Banking Sector

The LBS now comprises the Central Bank of Libya, sixteen commercial banks, specialized banks and an offshore bank. A number of foreign banks also have offices in the country (CBL 2010a).

3.3.2.1 Central Bank of Libya

The Central Bank of Libya represents the executive authority and is at the top of the banking hierarchy. Established in 1955, it started its activities in 1956 with a capital of 500 million Libyan dinars. The Libyan Banking Law (Law No.1/2005) set out the tasks of the bank, which include issuing currency, controlling and organizing credit, supervising and monitoring Libya's banks and formulating fiscal policy. It is responsible for the state's banking, for managing the state's reserves and for maintaining a stable exchange rate (CBL 2010a).

3.3.2.2 Commercial Banks

Libya's commercial banks are joint-stock companies and include private banks, state banks and those with mixed ownership. A number of foreign banks and financial institutions invest in Libyan commercial banks, though the number of shares they may hold is limited by law. Commercial banks provide a range of banking services, such as taking deposits from savers and investors, opening documentary credits, collecting banking instruments, granting credit facilities, issuing guarantees, and money exchange services. In recent years, they have also begun to offer a range of Islamic financial services (CBL 2010a).

The CBL's efforts to restructure Libya's banking system are geared towards creating banking institutions that can compete internationally. To this end, it has merged some commercial banks, raised the minimum amount of capital commercial banks are required to hold and diversified bank ownership, even to the point of relinquishing some of its own shares to allow foreign investors to own shares in commercial banks. Table 3.2 summarizes the current ownership structure in Libya's commercial banks.

3.3.3 The Legal Framework for the Libyan Banking Sector

The first legislation governing the banking sector was issued in 1958. This was followed by further legislation in 1963, 1993 and 2005, the last of which was amended in Law No.46/2012. Law No.1/2005 comprises four chapters addressing the nature and functions of the CBL, its role in establishing and supervising banks, the penalties for breaking the law, and articles relating to Islamic banking. The 2012 amendments, which were introduced in response to the significant changes in the Libyan legal framework and Libyan culture as a whole, include a new chapter on Islamic

Table 3.2: Ownership Structure in Libya's Commercial Banks.

No	Name of bank	Establishment date	Public	Private	Foreign partner	Total
1	Jumhoriya Bank	1969	90.26%	9.74%	0.00%	100%
2	Sahara Bank	1964	59.00%	22.00%	19.00%	100%
3	National Commercial Bank	1970	85.00%	15.00%	0.00%	100%
4	Wahada Bank	1970	63.00%	19.00%	18.00%	100%
5	North Africa Bank	1997	82.00%	18.00%	0.00%	100%
6	Commerce & Development Bank	1995	17.00%	49.00%	34.00%	100%
7	Al-Waha Bank	2006	100.00%	0.00%	0.00%	100%
8	Al-Amman Bank	2003	40.00%	60.00%	0.00%	100%
9	United Bank	2007	3.00%	57.00%	40.00%	100%
10	Arab Commercial Bank	2007	0.00%	0.00%	100.00%	100%
11	Al-Saraya Bank	2007	0.00%	100.00%	0.00%	100%
12	Al-Ejmaa Alarabi Bank	2004	0.00%	100.00%	0.00%	100%
13	Mediterranean Bank	2006	0.00%	100.00%	0.00%	100%
14	Al-Wafa Bank	2004	0.72%	99.28%	0.00%	100%
15	First Gulf Libyan Bank	2008	50.00%	0.00%	50.00%	100%
16	Al-Nuran Bank[1]	2008	50.00%	0.00%	50.00%	100%

Source: CBL (2012)

banking and changes relating to corporate governance. For example, while Article 68 of the 2005 law states that commercial banks must be managed by a board of between five and seven members, in the 2012 law, the maximum number is raised to nine. The new law also stipulates that board members should have five years' experience, rather than the previous requirement that they should simply have "sufficient" experience. While the 2005 law requires institutions controlled by the CBL to disclose their most recent financial statement at some point in the year in the national and local press, the new law adds that it should also be disclosed on the institution's website. Article 86 of the 2005 law states that in banks controlled by the CBL, shareholders owning a 25% stake and depositors who have deposits equal to 25% of the bank's total deposits can ask the CBL to inspect and monitor the bank. The new law reduces this to 10%.

Since commercial banks are joint-stock companies, they must also comply with the Libyan Commercial Law, most recently updated in 2010. This law covers all aspects of commercial activity in Libya, including corporate governance. However, the main authority in respect of corporate governance in commercial banks is the mandatory Corporate Governance Code for Libyan Banks (CGLBS), issued in 2010 (replacing the voluntary code of 2006). The mechanisms of this code and other related codes and legislation are the focus of Section 3.4 of this review.

1 Al-Nuran Bank was established in 2008 but did not become operational until 2015.

3.3.4 Reform and Privatization in the Libyan Banking Sector

The government's privatization policy was prompted by reports from a variety of institutions and experts describing widespread stagnation and corruption under the communist economic model. Bengdara (2007, p. 2) argues that prior to privatization, partial or complete ownership by the CBL adversely affected the performance of commercial banks in several ways:

- The banks were tied up by regulatory restrictions and red tape, with decisions needing to be ratified by several different people.
- The overly bureaucratic environment weakened management performance.
- Employees lacked financial incentives.
- Many branches had been established in regions that didn't warrant them, in order to appease tribal sensitivities. This led to many branches going bankrupt.
- As productivity rates declined, overstaffing increased.
- The banks were obliged to grant loans to companies in the public sector without conducting feasibility studies or obtaining sufficient guarantees.

In response, the government adopted a series of economic reforms, including privatization. Law No.1/1993 was the first step towards privatizing the banking sector; this law allowed the establishment of local, private banks and permitted foreign banks to open offices and branches in Libya (CBL 2010b). As a result of this law, a number of commercial banks were established, including the Commerce and Development Bank in 1996, the Mediterranean Bank and the Al-Saraya Bank in 1997, the Al-Ejmaa Alarabi Bank in 2003 and the Al-Wafa Bank in 2004 (CBL 2006). This was followed by Law No.1/2005, which represented a quantum leap in terms of reform. Not only did Article 72 of the law allow individuals and institutions to buy shares in state-owned banks, but the law also opened the sector up to foreign investors, allowing the CBL to establish banks with foreign capital and permitting foreign banks to buy up to US$15 million worth of shares in domestic banks and to open their own branches in Libya. In 2010, the CBL announced in its annual report that it would issue licences to two foreign banks permitting them to acquire up to 49% ownership of the new banks, giving them full management control. The remaining 51% would be owned by domestic investors. The CBL asserted that it would handle all issues related to the issuance of the two licences and mobilize domestic investors (CBL 2010a). In the same year, the CBL sold 15% of its shares in the National Commercial Bank on the LSM (ibid).

3.4 Corporate Governance in Libya

Corporate governance in Libya is still in its early stages. Aspects of corporate governance in the banking sector are covered by the Libyan Banking Law (Law No.1/

2005) and its 2012 amendments, and by the Libyan Commercial Law of 2010. The first corporate governance code was issued by the CBL in 2006. However, this code was non-mandatory, and Libyan banks generally failed to comply with most of its recommendations. A second corporate governance code was issued by the LSM in 2007, but it too was non-mandatory. This code sought to promote responsible and transparent management behaviour in joint-stock companies listed on the LSM and to bring Libyan corporate governance into line with international best practice (CGLSM2007). In 2010, the CBL replaced the 2006 guidelines with a mandatory code. This has six parts: the definition of corporate governance; shareholders' rights; the board of directors; committees of the board of directors; disclosure; and other requirements (CGLBS2010). This section discusses how these various laws and codes deal with the mechanisms of corporate governance. Table 3.3 presents a comparative overview of these codes and laws.

3.4.1 The Board of Directors

3.4.1.1 Type of Board

According to Libyan Commercial Law No.23/2010, shareholders must appoint a board made up of executive and non-executive directors (NEDs) to take overall responsibility for running the company. Although the Commercial Law stipulates that the board should be unitary, it permits the board to delegate some of its powers to an executive committee consisting of one or more board members to act on its behalf. This suggests that the law allows companies to follow either the unitary or the dual board model in practice. Regarding the delegation of authority to executive committees, the CGLSM (2007) cautions that

> [t]he board of directors holds all authority for controlling the company and remains ultimately responsible, even where it has established committees or authorized other entities or individuals to carry out certain tasks. The board must avoid issuing warrants that are general or unspecified in duration. (CGLSM2007, p. 10)

The 2006 and 2010 CGLBS, the 2005 Banking Law and its 2012 amendment all adopt the dual board model (see Table 3.3). Libya thus differs from Anglo-Saxon countries such as the UK and the US, which follow unitary board, shareholder-oriented models of corporate governance (Mallin 2007; Solomon 2013; Gup 2007). Instead, it seems more influenced by Germany, Austria, the Netherlands, Denmark and Japan, which follow dual board, stakeholder-oriented models, and by France and Switzerland, which allow both unitary board and dual board models (Maw, Lane of Horse, Craig-Cooper and Alsbury 1994; Hopt and Leyens 2004; Gup 2007).

Table 3.3: Comparison of Corporate Governance Initiatives in Libya.

	Libyan Banking Law (2005)	Amendments to the Banking Law (2012)	CGLBS (2006)	Libyan Commercial Law (2010)	CGLSM (2007)	CGLBS (2010)
Unitary or dual board of directors	Dual board	No amendments	Dual board	Unitary and dual board	Dual board	Dual board
Separation of Chairperson and CEO	Not combined	No amendments	Not combined	Combined or separate	Not combined	Not combined
Non-executive directors	The majority of board members must be NEDs.	No amendments	No more than one or two executive directors	Executive but can delegate power to committees.	The majority of board members should be NEDs.	The majority of board members must be NEDs.
Independent non-executive directors	Not mentioned	No amendments	No less than two should be independent. Independence should be clearly determined.	Not mentioned	Two or one-third of the board should be independent, whichever is greater. Independence should be clearly determined.	No less than two should be independent. Independence should be clearly determined.
Size of board of directors	7–9 members	9 members at least	Small enough to allow for accountability but big enough to ensure variety.	Not mentioned	3–11	7–9

(continued)

Table 3.3 (continued)

	Libyan Banking Law (2005)	**Amendments to the Banking Law (2012)**	**CGLBS (2006)**	**Libyan Commercial Law (2010)**	**CGLSM (2007)**	**CGLBS (2010)**
Role of board of directors	Not mentioned	No amendments	Required to be honest, loyal and committed to the bank.	Board members should carry out their duties carefully, in accordance with the company's articles of association.	The board of directors should carry out its duties responsibly and in good faith, and with seriousness and attention.	The board of directors must carry out its responsibilities in accordance with the power given to the board under the bank statute and the relevant laws and legislation.
Appointment of board of directors	Appointed by the bank's general assembly. The board must select the chairperson from among its members.	Appointed by the bank's general assembly. The board must elect the chairperson and one or more vice-chairperson from among its members.	Not mentioned	Appointed by the general assembly of shareholders.	The general assembly should appoint board members for the period stipulated in the statute, provided this does not exceed three years, and may re-appoint members unless the statute dictates otherwise.	Appointed by the bank's general assembly. The board should select the chairperson from among its members.

Compensation of board of directors	By the company's general assembly	No amendments	By the remuneration committee	Determined by the company's articles of association.	Non-cash benefits and/or a percentage of the company profits. Board members may receive two or more forms of compensation.	Non-cash benefits and/or a percentage of the company profits. Board members may receive two or more forms of compensation, as decided by the general assembly and remuneration committee.
Board committees	The bank must outsource the task of mortgage assessment to specialist agencies and set up a compliance unit, to be supervised by the board.	Not mentioned	Recommends audit, remuneration and risk committees.	Stipulates a monitoring committee of three members.	Recommends companies to establish a control committee of not less than three members, to be appointed by the general assembly.	Requires audit, remuneration, risk management and governance committees.
Shareholders' and stakeholders' rights	Basic shareholders' rights	Not mentioned	Not mentioned	Basic shareholders' rights	Extensive details	Extensive details

(continued)

Table 3.3 (continued)

	Libyan Banking Law (2005)	**Amendments to the Banking Law (2012)**	**CGLBS (2006)**	**Libyan Commercial Law (2010)**	**CGLSM (2007)**	**CGLBS (2010)**
Disclosure and transparency	Financial information	Not mentioned	Recommends disclosure of financial and regulatory information and executive managers' remuneration.	Requires disclosure of financial information but no mention of corporate governance disclosure.	Recommends policies and procedures of disclosure and supervisory regulations in written form in accordance with rules determined by the market.	Stipulates for shareholders: operational and financial findings; strategic objectives; board and managers' information; corporate governance practice; dealings with related parties; human resources. For stakeholders: financial reports; management information. For CBL: additional corporate governance information. For LSM: disclosure requirements in LSM.

3.4.1.2 Board Composition

3.4.1.2.1 Separation of Chairperson and CEO

Separation between the chairperson and CEO is required in both CGLBS codes and the Libyan Banking Law. The CGLSM also requires that the board chairman should have no executive function. In contrast, the Libyan Commercial Law of 2010 states that the board can appoint a general manager from among its members or from outside and that it can appoint assistant managers and administrative officers according to the articles of association. In other words, under this law, the roles of chairperson and CEO can be combined. The separation requirement is consistent with codes in developed countries; the UK Corporate Governance Code (2010) (formerly the Combined Code), for example, recommends that the positions and responsibilities of the chairperson and CEO should be separated, while the OECD advises that separating the two roles enhances corporate accountability:

> Separation of the two posts may be regarded as good practice, as it can help to achieve an appropriate balance of power, increase accountability and improve the board's capacity for decision making independent of management. (OECD 2004, p. 63)

3.4.1.2.2 Non-executive Directors

The CGLSM(2007), the Libyan Banking Law (2005) and the CGLBS(2010) all require the majority of board members to be non-executive. The 2006 CGLBS code stipulates no more than one or two executive directors on the board. In contrast, the Libyan Commercial Law (2010) permits the majority of board members to be executives. The general requirement that the majority of board members should be NEDs is consistent with expectations in developed countries; the Basel Committee on Banking Supervision (BCBS), for instance, explains the importance of NEDs thus:

> Independence and objectivity can be enhanced by including qualified nonexecutive directors on the board or by having a supervisory board or board of auditors separate from a management board. This is particularly important in areas where there is a risk that the board of directors would be dominated by senior management or political influences, where there are influences on the board to take action that is not in the bank's best interest (although it may be in the personal interest of insiders or major shareholders), or where there is a potential for conflict of interest in key areas. (BCBS 2006, p. 7)

3.4.1.2.3 Independent Non-Executive Directors

The Libyan Commercial Law (2010) and the Libyan Banking Law (2005) are both silent in relation to director independence. In contrast, the 2006 and 2010 CGLBS codes both state that no fewer than two of the permanent board members should be independent. The codes identify several factors that may affect board members' independence:

- Personality clashes between members
- The existence of a supervisory relationship
- The existence of a direct or indirect commercial relationship between a board member and the bank
- Any new relationship that develops as a consequence of board membership (CGLBS 2010, p.7)

The CGLSM states that "[t]here must be two independent board members, or independents must make up one-third of the members of the board, whichever is greater" (CGLSM (2007, p. 9) and that

> [t]he chairman and members of the board of directors are not allowed to have any direct or indirect interest in the company's business. The chairman and members of the board of directors and managers are not allowed to participate in any action that might bring them into competition with the company. (CGLSM 2007, p. 9)

The CGLBS and CGLSM codes echo international corporate governance codes in asserting the importance of having independent NEDs on the board. The OECD explains that this is because

> [i]ndependent board members can contribute significantly to the decision making of the board. They can bring an objective view to the evaluation of the performance of the board and management. In addition, they can play an important role in areas where the interests of management, the company and its shareholders may diverge such as executive remuneration, succession planning, changes of corporate control, take-over defences, large acquisitions and the audit function. In order for them to play this key role, it is desirable that boards declare who they consider to be independent and the criterion for this judgement. (OECD 2004, p. 64)

Basel Committee on Banking Supervision BCBS emphasises the particular importance of board member independence in banks with the stipulation that

> banks should have an adequate number and appropriate composition of directors who are capable of exercising judgment independent of the views of management, political interests or inappropriate outside interests. (BCBS 2006, p. 7)

3.4.1.3 Board Size

The Libyan Commercial Law (2010) does not specify how many directors are required, but the CGLSM (2007) recommends that the board should have between three and eleven members. The Libyan Banking Law (2005) and CGLBS (2010) require between seven and nine members, while the 2012 amendment raises the size of the board to at least nine members. Libya's laws and codes thus follow corporate governance codes in developed countries in recommending that boards should not be too large. The UK corporate governance Code (2010), for instance, advises that board size should not be so large as to be unwieldy.

3.4.1.4 Role of Board of Directors

The Libyan Banking Law (2005) does not address the role of the board of directors at all, and the other codes do so only in general terms. Thus, the CGLSM (2007) states that "[t]he board of directors should carry out its duties responsibly and in good faith, and with seriousness and attention, and its decisions should be based on adequate information from the executive management, or any other reliable source" (CGLSM 2007, p. 6). The Libyan Commercial Law (2010) stipulates that board members should carry out their duties carefully in accordance with the company's articles of association, while the 2010 CGLBS code says the board must carry out its responsibilities in accordance with the power given to it under the bank statute and the relevant laws and legislation. corporate governance codes in developed countries provide more specific details about the board's role; according to the UK corporate governance Code,

> [t]he board's role is to provide entrepreneurial leadership of the company within a framework of prudent and effective controls which enables risk to be assessed and managed. The board should set the company's strategic aims, ensure that the necessary financial and human resources are in place for the company to meet its objectives and review management performance. The board should set the company's values and standards and ensure that its obligations to its shareholders and others are understood and met.
>
> (UK corporate governance Code 2010, p. 3)

The OECD's Principles of Corporate Governance (2004) list the responsibilities of the board under six headings: monitoring of management, duty of care and loyalty, ethical standards, key functions, corporate affairs, and access to information.

3.4.1.5 Appointment of the Board of Directors

The Libyan Banking Law (2005) and 2010 CGLBS code require the board of directors to be appointed by the bank's general assembly. The board should then select its chairperson from among its members. Law No.46/2012 adds that the board should also elect one or more vice-chairs. The Libyan Commercial Law (2010) states that if the arrangements for appointing the board are not set out in the company's bylaws, it should be appointed by the general assembly. Directors may serve for three years unless the company articles stipulate otherwise, and the general assembly may dismiss part or all of the board. The CGLSM code advises that

> [t]he general assembly should appoint members of the board of directors for the period stipulated in the statute, provided this does not exceed three years, and may reappoint members of the board of directors unless the statute dictates otherwise. (CGLSM 2007, p. 14)

Codes in developed countries (e.g. UK Corporate Governance Code, 2010; OECD 2004; Basel Committee on Banking Supervision 2006) require the appointment process to be overseen by a nomination committee to ensure that a suitable balance of skills and experience is maintained within the company and on the board.

3.4.1.6 Compensation of the Board of Directors

The Libyan Banking Law (2005) says only that board compensation should be determined by the general assembly. In contrast, the Libyan Commercial Law (2010) stipulates that board compensation should be determined in the company's articles of association. The CGLSM (2007) states that

> [t]he general assembly should determine the level and structure of compensation for board members. This compensation may be paid as a defined remuneration, an allowance for attending meetings, non-cash benefits or a percentage of the company profits. Members may receive two or more of these forms of compensation. (CGLSM 2007, p. 12)

The 2006 CGLBS code's recommendation that the board should set up a remuneration committee is retained in the 2010 version of the code this makes the general assembly responsible for determining the financial benefits to be given to board members (including the chairperson), based on the recommendations of the remuneration committee. These financial benefits may take the form of a percentage of the bank profits or other benefits recommended by the committee. International codes such as the UK corporate governance code (2010) stipulate that the remuneration committee should be made up of independent NEDs, and that remuneration should be performance-based. Basel Committee on Banking Supervision indicates that

> [t]he remuneration committee is responsible for providing oversight of remuneration of senior management and other key personnel and ensuring that compensation is consistent with the bank's culture, objectives, strategy and control environment. (BCBS 2006, p. 8)

3.4.1.7 Board Committees

The Libyan Banking Law (2005) does not mention audit committees. In regard to risk management, it states that the bank should outsource the task of assessing mortgages to outside specialists, and set up a compliance unit, to be supervised by the board. The 2006 CGLBS code advises boards to delegate authority to audit, remuneration and risk committees to increase board efficiency, while the Libyan Commercial Law (2010) requires general assemblies to appoint a monitoring committee of at least three members, at least one of whom should be university qualified.

The CGLSM (2007) pays significant attention to the audit committee, recommending that

> [t]he board of directors should constitute a committee from non-executive members to be called the audit committee. It should have no fewer than three members, at least one of whom should be competent in finance and accounting. The board of directors should issue rules for

> the selection of members to the audit committee, their length of tenure and the committee's method of working. (CGLSM 2007, p. 10)

The code sets out the committee's tasks and responsibilities as being:
- To supervise the company's internal audit department and verify its effectiveness in carrying out the tasks delegated to it by the board of directors
- To examine the internal control system and present a written report detailing its views and recommendations
- To examine the internal audit reports and ensure that any corrective actions recommended therein are implemented
- To make recommendations to the board of directors regarding the appointment and dismissal of external auditors and the fees to be paid; to ensure the independence of these auditors
- To monitor the external auditor, particularly if they take any action outside the scope of the work originally assigned to them
- To review the audit plan with the external auditor and make comments on it; to review the external auditor's comments on the financial statements and follow-up thereon
- To review the financial statements before submission to the board of directors and to express an opinion and recommendations in respect thereof
- To study the company's accounting policies and give opinions and recommendations in respect thereof

The CGLSM (2007) also advises companies to establish a control committee of not less than three members, to be appointed by the general assembly. According to the code, "[t]he committee should have all the rights and responsibilities set out in the Libyan Commercial Law" (CGLSM 2007, p. 10). Its tasks include: overseeing the management's actions in order to ensure that they are legal, ensuring the validity of company contracts and their legitimacy, reviewing and auditing the company accounts, as prescribed by the law, and ensuring that all accounting procedures are in accordance with legal and regulatory rules. The members of the control committee have the right to inspect the company and its work and to ask managers for information about any of its operations. All of the committee's investigations and inquiries must be documented and stored in a special archive.

Finally, the CGLBS (2010) stipulates that banks must have audit, remuneration, risk management and governance committees. It describes the responsibilities of the audit committee as including: reviewing and auditing bank processes; liaising between directors and external auditors; and submitting a quarterly report about its activities to the board. It can be concluded that most corporate governance codes and laws in Libya require the establishment of board committees, particularly audit committees. This is consistent with corporate governance codes in developed countries (UK corporate governance Code 2010; OECD 2004; Basel Committee on Banking Supervision (2006).

3.4.2 Shareholders' and Stakeholders' Rights

The CGLSM (2007) provides extensive details about shareholders' rights, explaining their right to have access to information, their rights in terms of general assembly meetings and their voting and dividend rights. CGLBS (2010), meanwhile, devotes a whole chapter to shareholder rights, covering issues around stock ownership, the rights of shareholders in the general assembly and the rights of minority shareholders. More limited information is given in the Libyan Commercial Law (2010) this covers shareholders' right to force the board to convene a general assembly meeting, their rights at this meeting, their right to deputize someone else to attend in their place, and their rights in the event of conflicts of interest arising between shareholders.

This emphasis on shareholders' rights as a key principle of corporate governance is in line with international codes, which deal at length with the issue. The OECD Principles, for example, assert that

> [t]he corporate governance framework should recognise the rights of stakeholders established by law or through mutual agreements and encourage active cooperation between corporations and stakeholders in creating wealth, jobs, and the sustainability of financially sound enterprises. (OECD 2004, p. 46)

3.4.3 Disclosure and Transparency Requirements

This section discusses the requirements set out in the various codes and legislation in respect of disclosure and transparency. As discussed in Section 3.4, commercial banks in the LBS are ruled primarily by the mandatory CGLBS (2010) code, with banks listed in the LSM also being expected to adhere to the voluntary CGLSM (2007) code. Both of these codes contain extensive disclosure and transparency requirements. More limited requirements exist within the Libyan Banking Law (2005) and the Libyan Commercial Law (2010).

3.4.3.1 The Financial and Operating Results of the Company

All of the codes and regulation require banks to disclose their financial information. Article 26 of the Libyan Banking Law (2005) requires banks to prepare and disclose financial statements in line with international standards, while the Libyan Commercial Law (2010) stipulates that the company management (board or managers) must provide the financial results to the external auditor within 60 days of the end of the financial year, and that the external auditor must provide their report to shareholders within 45 days. The CGLSM[2] (2007) requires listed companies to disclose their annual and half-annual financial statements, along with the notes and the external auditor's report, in two daily popular journals one in English and the other in Arabic within a week of adoption by the AGM.

Finally, the CGLBS (2010) requires banks to fully disclose their financial information to stakeholders and shareholders in the AGM. This information should include the income statement, financial position statement, cash flow statement and change in equity statement. Banks are also required to disclose the notes to the financial statement, as stipulated in the IAS, and information on how managers have dealt with these notes. This is consistent with the OECD Principles (2004), which identify the disclosure of financial information as one of the most important T&D requirements. This requires the production and dissemination of audited financial statements showing the financial performance and financial situation of the company (these typically include the balance sheet, the profit and loss statement, the cash flow statement and accompanying notes). This information is central to corporate governance as it enables stakeholders to monitor the company's performance; as the OECD puts it: "Failures of governance can often be linked to the failure to disclose the whole picture." (OECD 2004, p. 49)

3.4.3.2 Bank Objectives and Non-financial Information

As far as non-financial information is concerned, the CGLBS (2010) requires banks to disclose information about their strategic plan and objectives, and how the board proposes to respond to the financial results. They should also set out their policy regarding social issues e.g. any donations and contributions to charities or social enterprises and their ethics charter. This governs how the bank deals with stakeholders and its position on human rights. The OECD Principles (2004) also encourage companies to disclose both their financial and non-financial objectives. This may include revealing details of their policies and performance in the areas of business ethics, the environment and, where relevant, social issues, human rights and other public policy commitments.

3.4.3.3 Major Share Ownership, Including Beneficial Owners, and Voting Rights

The OECD Principles (2004) advise that details about ownership may include an explanation of the structure of the enterprise and shareholders' rights vis-à-vis the rights of other owners. Where the company is part of a group, disclosure may cover how this group is structured and describe intra-group relations. It may also include

2 Only seven out of the sixteen LCBs are listed in the LSM (Jumhoriya Bank, Sahara Bank, National Commercial Bank, Wahada Bank, Commerce and Development Bank, Mediterranean Bank, Al-Saraya Bank).

information about the shareholdings of directors, including non-executives, and beneficial owners Companies listed in the LSM are expected to disclose any changes in the shareholder base where this means there is a new majority shareholder (CGLSM 2007).The CGLBS (2010), meanwhile, requires banks to disclose information to stakeholders about anyone owning more than 5% of the bank's capital. If another company owns shares in the bank, the bank should also disclose information about this company and how many shares it owns to both shareholders and the general public.

3.4.3.4 Remuneration of Members of the Board and Key Executives

According to the OECD (2004), companies should disclose information about the remuneration of individual board members and key executives. Similarly, the CGLSM (2007) expects listed companies to disclose details about the remuneration of every board member plus the five highest-paid executives. The CGLBS (2010) requires commercial banks only to disclose information about the salaries, benefits and rewards given to board members, though they are also expected to make clear how remuneration is linked to board performance.

3.4.3.5 Information About Board Members

The OECD (2004) advises that information about board members should include their qualifications, their share ownership in the company, their membership of other boards, any other executive positions, and whether they are considered independent members of the board.

The CGLSM (2007, p. 5) requires banks to provide a full list of the names and titles/roles of all board members. Where these board members also sit on the boards of other companies, the bank is expected to name these companies. The CGLBS (2010, p. 39) goes further, stipulating that the information disclosed should include: personal information about every board member and a summary of their CV showing their experience and qualifications; the proportion of their shares in the bank; their membership of other boards; whether they are considered by the board to be an independent member; and how they were elected. This information should be made available to stakeholders, shareholders and the public.

3.4.3.6 Related Party Transactions

According to the OECD (2004), all material related party transactions and the terms of such transactions should be individually disclosed. The Principles add that "[i]n case the jurisdiction does not define materiality, companies should be required to also disclose the policy/criteria adopted for determining material related party transactions" (OECD 2004, p. 52). Related parties should, at minimum, include entities that control or are under common control with the company, significant shareholders (including members of their families) and key management personnel

Under the CGLBS (2010), banks must disclose to stakeholders their policies regarding conflicts of interest. They must also reveal the conditions, specifications and value of all related party transactions.

3.4.3.7 Foreseeable Risk Factors

These may include risks that are specific to the industry or the geographical area(s) in which the company operates; risk arising from the company's dependence on certain commodities; financial market risks including interest rate or currency risk; risk related to derivatives and off-balance sheet transactions; risk arising from the routine conduct of business; and environmental risks such as natural disasters. The OECD (2004) insists that disclosure of this information is very important for users and market participants.

The CGLBS (2010) also requires banks to disclose information to stakeholders regarding foreseeable risk factors and how these might be mitigated or avoided. This includes details of the bank's risk policies, the structure of the predicted risks and the bank's procedures for managing them.

3.4.3.8 Issues Regarding Employees and Other Stakeholders

The CGLBS (2010) requires banks to disclose not just their general human resource policy, but also more specific information on matters such as recruitment mechanisms, training programmes, salaries and labour turnover rates.

3.4.3.9 Governance Structures and Policies

According to the OECD (2004), companies should disclose details of their corporate governance practice, particularly the division of authority between shareholders, management and board members. Companies should also ensure that shareholder votes are properly counted and recorded and that the results are announced promptly. Banks listed in the LSM are expected to disclose information demonstrating their compliance with the requirements of the listing list along with the reasons for any non-compliance (CGLSM 2007). The CGLBS (2010), meanwhile, requires banks to disclose details of their corporate governance structure (including board structure and committees, how these are regulated and how the board assesses corporate governance effectiveness in the bank), their charter of ethics, their organisational structure and main activities. They must also list the institutions with which they are linked, giving details of each institution's location and main activities and the bank's shareholding.

3.4.3.10 Quality of Accounting and Financial and Non-financial Reporting

The OECD (2004) advises that the adoption of high-quality standards increases the reliability and comparability of reports, allowing investors to monitor the company more effectively. Accordingly, the CGLBS (2010) stipulates that the financial statement should comply with international standards of accounting and auditing, and that listed banks should adhere to the disclosure requirements of the LSM.

3.4.3.11 Auditing

The OECD (2004) states that

> [a]n annual audit should be conducted by an independent, competent and qualified auditor in order to provide an external and objective assurance to the board and shareholders that the financial statements fairly represent the financial position and performance of the company in all material respects [...] The external auditors should be accountable to the shareholders and owe a duty to the company to exercise due professional care in the conduct of the audit.
>
> (OECD 2004, p. 54)

It continues: "The external auditors should be accountable to the shareholders and owe a duty to the company to exercise due professional care in the conduct of the audit." (OECD 2004, p. 54)

The Libyan Banking Law (2005) stipulates that the accounting reports of state banks must be audited by the Libyan Audit Bureau in accordance with the rules of the CBL and international auditing and accounting standards. The CGLSM (2007) requires listed companies to disclose the results of the annual audit of the efficiency of internal control procedures in the company. Finally, the CGLBS (2010) stipulates that copies of all committee reports, including those of the audit committee, must be submitted to the CBL within five days of being presented to the board.

3.4.3.12 Channels for Disseminating Information

Under the CGLBS (2010), banks must disclose their management and financial information to all stakeholders including depositors, investors and the public. The information should be presented in an annual report and either posted on the bank's website or printed out and left in the reception area of the bank where it can be seen by stakeholders. This is in line with the OECD's (2004) recommendation that "[c]hannels for disseminating information should provide for equal, timely and cost efficient access to relevant information by users" (OECD 2004, p. 56). Acknowledging that investors may need help interpreting this information, the Principles also advise that

> [t]he corporate governance framework should be complemented by an effective approach that addresses and promotes the provision of analysis or advice by analysts, brokers, rating agencies and others, that is relevant to decisions by investors and free from material conflicts of interest that might compromise the integrity of their analysis or advice.
>
> (OECD 2004, p. 56)

3.5 Summary

This chapter presents a general overview of the Libyan context. It describes Libya's demographic characteristics, including population, language and geography, before discussing its recent political and economic development and the major changes that have taken place (and continue to take place) in the country. The discussion reveals that since the 1960s, Libya's economic progress, which has been almost entirely dependent on its oil industry, has been closely linked to political developments in the country. This progress suffered between 1969 and 1987 under the Gaddafi regime's nationalisation policy, started to show signs of improvement when this policy was replaced by a programme of liberalisation, but is once more suffering under the turbulence that has afflicted the country since the popular revolution of 2011. At the time of writing, the Libyan business environment continues to be negatively impacted by Gaddafi's legacy of corruption, lack of democracy and rule of law, and a restricted press.

The chapter shows that Libya differs from developed countries in being profoundly influenced firstly, by Islam, which has occupied a central position in all of its constitutions and which is, through Islamic Sharia, the main inspiration behind the country's legislation, and secondly, by the importance it attaches to kinship ties. This emphasis on kinship and family/tribal loyalty affects the business environment in numerous ways; for example, unqualified individuals are appointed to positions of importance through nepotism, the independence of auditors and board members is undermined, and the pressure for disclosure is reduced. There are thus several points of difference between Libya and developed countries, but the chapter goes on to show that since the revolution, Libya has also diverged from the other Arab Spring countries in the sense that it is the only one of the five to see the old regime fall and not be replaced by a new national government. The continuing instability and the separation of governance in Libya has affected all sectors, including the banking sector, with the result that the economy has sustained much greater damage than those of Tunisia or Egypt.

The chapter then moves on to Libya's banking sector, providing a review of the historical development of the sector and a discussion of its current structure, the legal framework governing banks, and the recent reforms. Identifying the key pieces of legislation and codes that address corporate governance in the LBS, the chapter compares these laws and codes in terms of their recommendations/stipulations regarding the board of directors and its committees, shareholder/stakeholder rights and T&D. The discussion shows that despite the unique nature of the Libyan context, Libyan corporate governance seems to have been impacted by and have multiple points of similarity with the codes that have been produced in developed countries and by international bodies such as the OECD.

This chapter introduces the key mechanisms of corporate governance disclosure and practice and the institutions that may be affecting the operation of these mechanisms within the Libyan context. The next chapter discusses the theoretical framework of corporate governance.

4 The Corporate Governance Theoretical Framework

4.1 Introduction

Henderksen defines theory as “a coherent set of hypotheticals, conceptual and pragmatic principles forming the general framework of reference for a field of inquiry” (Henderksen 1970, p. 1). Such a framework is essential for understanding corporate governance and related issues. Ziolkowski advises that

> [c]orporate governance research should be no different from scholarly inquiries in natural science in terms of methodological approach. Such research requires that corporate governance scholars place the subjective process of developing ideas into a logical framework of challenge and questioning through debate and data collection. This is a continuous process starting with conceptual and propositional analysis for defining terms, model building and theory development. (Ziolkowski 2005, pp. 357–358)

An understanding of the theories that have been employed to investigate corporate governance is therefore a useful place to start.

This chapter begins by reviewing the main theories that have been used to interpret corporate governance in the literature and explaining why they were unsuitable in this case. It then describes the institutional theory framework as an alternative framework that can be used to interpret corporate governance in a Libyan context. It briefly introducing the different forms of institutional theory that have emerged, some of the key ways in which the theory has been developed by researchers, and its associated concepts. The chapter ends by discussing the main institutions that may shape corporate governance disclosure and practice in Libya.

4.2 Theoretical Frameworks Traditionally used to interpret Corporate Governance

The theories that have dominated corporate governance research include stewardship theory, agency theory, transaction cost theory and stakeholder theory. The following sections discuss these theories in order to provide a better understanding of why they are not suitable for corporate governance in Libyan context.

4.2.1 Stewardship Theory

Deriving from the disciplines of psychology and sociology, stewardship theory views executives as stewards working on behalf of their principals (Davis,

https://doi.org/10.1515/9783110602111-004

Schoorman and Donaldson 1997; Donaldson and Davis 1991). Unlike agency theory, which expects agents to behave opportunistically, stewardship theory posits that because they share the same objectives as their principals, they are motivated to protect their interests (Bareney 1990; Donaldson and Davis 1991; Donaldson 1990a, 1990b). Donaldson and Davis (1991) explain that, to the steward, "pro-organisational, collectivistic behaviours have higher utility than individualistic, self-serving behaviours" (Donaldson and Davis 1991, p. 24). In other words, managers are team players and there is no conflict of interest between them and shareholders. According to Davis, Schoorman and Donaldson (1997), the steward's interests align with those of shareholders because, by protecting the latters' wealth, the steward maximizes his own utility and makes himself indispensable. Daily, Dalton and Canella (2003) suggest that stewards may also be driven by the desire to protect their own professional reputation.

Stakeholder theory's recognition of non-tangible motivations is noted by Agyris (1973), who argues that unlike agency theory, which sees employees in purely economic terms, stewardship theory recognizes the importance of structures that empower managers and offer them maximum autonomy built on trust. This was the vision at the heart of the joint-stock companies which emerged in the mid-ninetieth century. Tricker explains that "[c]lassical corporate governance, derived from the mid-nineteenth concept of the corporation, is rooted in the philosophy that men can be trusted; that directors can be relied on to act in the best interest of the company" (Tricker 1994, p. 3). However, this might be seen as a rather optimistic view. As Solomon and Martin note, in an imaginary world

> perhaps there would be no conflict of interest, no hard choices, no tragedies, and [...] people could fulfil both their desires and their responsibilities without adversely affecting anyone else. But that would just be an imaginary world [...] One person's gain is often another person's loss. One desire conflicts with another. (Solomon and Martin 2004, p. 70)

The pessimism expressed by Solomon and Martin seems justified when one considers the role executive opportunism has played in major corporate collapses such as those of Enron, WorldCom, HIH insurance, Global Crossing and Tyco International.

In Libya, the LSM's Corporate Governance Code (CGLSM 2007), the Libyan Banking Law (2005) and the 2010 corporate governance code (CGLBS 2010) all require the majority of board members to be non-executive, suggesting that Libya's regulators want to improve supervision and monitoring and strengthen management accountability. The emphasis on NEDs seems out of step with stewardship theory's assumption that managers are inherently trustworthy and do not need monitoring, but it may be seen as a response to the particular nature of the Libyan context, in which executives are often appointed because of their family or personal connections to the company rather than their experience and qualifications. Stewardship theory's assumptions about the skills and motivations of managers may therefore be misplaced when it comes to the Libyan banking sector, making it unsuitable as a theoretical basis for interpret corporate governance disclosure and practice in Libya.

4.2.2 Agency Theory

Agency theory was developed by Jensen and Meckling in 1976. According to Bricker and Chandar, "[c]urrent mainstream accounting research is based extensively on economic models of agency that represent the operating company (firm) manager as 'agent' and the individual investor as 'principal'" (Bricker and Chandar 1998, p. 478). The relationship between the two (the agency relationship) takes the form of "a contract under which one or more persons (the principal(s)) engage another person (the agent) to perform some service on their behalf which involves delegating some decision making authority to the agent" (Jensen and Meckling 1976, p. 308).

The central assumption of agency theory is that people are essentially self-interested and that as a result, whenever they engage in any cooperative action, conflicts of interest will inevitably arise (Agrawal and Knoeber 1996; Jensen 1994). Ittonen explains that this is likely to happen if "an individual or an organisation (an agent) has multiple interests and of those interests, one could possibly corrupt the motivation for an act in the other" (Ittonen 2010, p. 15). The main problem investigated by agency theory is the conflict of interest that arises between agent (manager) and principal (shareholder); that is, how the agent can be persuaded to act in the best interests of the principal (Sappington 1991), and how this relationship can be managed so as to achieve the best company performance. Agency problems arise when shareholders put pressure on managers to make decisions in line with their interests. These problems incur agency costs which, according to Jensen and Meckling (1976), may be divided into three categories: monitoring costs (costs incurred by shareholders to ensure that managers' actions are consistent with their interests), bonding costs (spending by managers to demonstrate that they are protecting shareholders' interests) and residual agency costs (incurred when monitoring and bonding costs alone fail to eliminate the conflict of interest and information asymmetry between agents and principals).

Solomon (2013) explains that the concept of corporate governance arose as a result of the agency problems caused by the separation of owners from the decision-making process. Hart (1995) also cites the conflict between owners and managers (or directors) as the main reason why corporate governance is so important in organisations, adding that contracts alone are insufficient to avert agency problems (not all business activities are conducted using a contract, and in any case, writing and enforcing contracts incurs significant agency costs). The agency problem is at the heart of Shleifer and Vishny (1997) argument that corporate governance is there to protect the interests of owners, and in the Cadbury Report's definition of corporate governance as a set of rules that separate control and ownership. Gillan and Starks (1998) offer a broader definition of corporate governance, explaining that

> [a]t one level, a firm's governance can be viewed as the set of structures that provides the boundaries for the operation of the enterprise. This entails not only participants, such as workers, managers, and suppliers of capital but also the returns to those participants and the constraints under which they operate. (Gillan and Starks 1998, p. 382)

Their definition recognizes the multiple relationships that impact on the firm's operations, from its relationships with its employees, investors, creditors, shareholders and other stakeholders to those with regulators and financial markets. Renders and Gaeremynck (2012) also highlight the impact of agency problems within principal-principal relationships; in a study covering listed companies from fourteen European countries over the period 1999–2003, they found that conflict within these relationships adversely affected the quality and effectiveness of corporate governance structures.

A problem with agency theory is that it does not take into account factors such as historical and cultural background or institutional arrangements, all of which may have an impact on corporate governance (Claessens and Laeven 2006). Germain, Galy and Lee (2014) criticise agency theory as inadequate for understanding corporate governance in Malaysian firms as there is no relationship between the measures under the monitoring hypothesis and board independence.

Pande and Ansari indicated that

> [t]he most popular theoretical framework, the agency theory, led to the evolution of the Anglo-Saxon model of corporate governance that is used widely to help the board of directors in curbing excessive executive power in the hands of management. However, with the blurring of the roles of the principal and the agent, the currently prevalent governance frameworks, based on this theory, have become self-limiting and ineffective. We need new theoretical insights that will take us towards a comprehensive theory of governance.
> (Pande and Ansari 2014, p. 56)

The Libyan government has taken a number of steps over recent years to reform corporate governance as part of its plan to promote privatization and encourage foreign investment. However, while significant reforms have already taken place in the LBS, the privatization programme is still in its early stages and state-owned banks still predominate. Since corporate governance codes in developed countries are generally designed with the intention of reducing agency conflicts in environments where ownership is dispersed and separated from control (Jensen and Meckling 1976), they may not be appropriate for the LBS, where dispersed ownership is not typical. Unlike developed countries, where corporate governance tends to be shaped by formal institutions such as the legal and regulatory framework, corporate governance in developing countries is more likely to be impacted by informal institutions such as kinship, religion, culture and politics. In these countries, legal and regulatory frameworks may be weak, ineffective or absent altogether (Young, Peng, Ahlstrom, Bruton and Jiang 2008). A major limitation of agency theory is that it takes no consideration of the role of these informal institutions.

4.2.3 Stakeholder Theory

According to the OECD, "[t]he corporate governance framework should recognise the rights of stakeholders established by law or through mutual agreements and encourage active cooperation between corporations and stakeholders in creating wealth, jobs, and the sustainability of financially sound enterprises" (OECD 2004, p. 21). Stakeholder theory was developed during the 1970s, but it was not until 1984 that Freeman proposed a general theory of the firm suggesting that corporations should consider themselves accountable to a broad range of stakeholders (Solomon 2013). Freeman (1984, p. 32) defined stakeholders as those individuals or groups who can affect or are affected by an organisation, but extreme proponents of stakeholder theory suggest that the environment, animal species and future generations should also be considered stakeholders. Donaldson and Preston take the highly inclusive view that "[s]takeholders are identified through the actual or potential harms and benefits that they experience or anticipate experiencing as a result of the firm's actions or inactions" (Donaldson and Preston 1995, p. 85).

According to stakeholder theory, a stakeholder is anyone with an interest in the organisation or who affects or is affected by its actions (Freeman and Vea 2001). The organisation's obligations, therefore, extend not just to shareholders but also customers, suppliers, employees, investors, lenders, auditors, government bodies and the community at large (Letza, Sun and Kirkbride 2004). Furthermore, the theory recognises that the actions of the firm may have not just financial but also social, economic, environmental and technological impacts (Clement 2005; Simmons 2004). For example, Ayuso, Rodríguez, García-Castro and Ariño (2014) argue that corporations facing crisis should balance their goal of maximising shareholder value against their moral responsibility towards other stakeholders such as employees and suppliers.

As far as corporate governance is concerned, stakeholder theory posits that companies must ensure that their governance meets the needs of all stakeholders (Clement 2005). Luoma and Goodstein (1999) indicate that some companies seek to do this by inviting customers, suppliers, employees and members of the public to sit on the board. However, very few countries have the legislation in place to make this kind of representation mandatory. The problem with stakeholder theory as a perspective for investigating corporate governance is that it is less developed than other theories; indeed, some have accused it of having little to offer in the way of insight into or suggestions for improving governance. Sternberg (1997), for example, is critical of stakeholder theory's assumption that corporations are equally accountable to all stakeholders. She argues that the theory ignores the primary aim of any business, which is to maximise long-term owner value, and assumes that the only way to achieve legitimacy is to balance the needs of all stakeholders, which is impossible.

4.2.4 Transaction Cost Theory

Williamson explains that transaction cost theory was developed to facilitate analysis of the "comparative costs of planning, adapting and monitoring task completion under alternative governance structures" (Williamson 1996, p. 22). He adds that a transaction occurs "when a good or service is transferred across a technologically separate interface". The theory assumes that companies get larger and more complicated as a result of external price changes which guide the production and the markets coordinate transaction (Solomon 2013). According to Williamson (1996), transaction costs are influenced by human and environmental factors: human factors include bounded rationality (the assumption that individuals lack the capacity or the resources to consider every state-contingent outcome of the transaction) and opportunism (self-interest as the motivation for work), while environmental factors include uncertainty, small numbers trading and asset specificity.

There are several studies investigating corporate governance from the perspective of transaction cost theory. Dittmar, Mahrt-Smith and Servaes (2003) for example, investigate the causes of transaction costs in countries with extensive shareholder protection, while Mayer and Solomon (2006) examine the impact of contractual hazards and technological capabilities on governance (finding that firms with strong technological capabilities are better able to control transaction costs), and Ezzamel and Willmott (1993) adopt transaction cost theory to investigate corporate governance in the UK's public sector. However, other researchers have criticized transaction cost theory as a perspective for investigating strategic and organisational issues. Ghoshal and Moran (1996), for example, argue that its underlying assumptions make it "dangerous" for executive managers. They also review other studies that criticize this theory (Dore 1983; Granovetter 1985; Perrow 1986; Simon 1991). Dore (1983) argues that ethnocentric bias undermines the generalizability of transaction cost theory, while Granovetter (1985) asserts that the theory pays too little attention to the contextual grounding of human actions, and Perrow (1986) suggests that it embodies a hidden ideology that distorts more than it illuminates. Williamson (1996) argues that in transaction cost economics, corporate governance is seen as having the twin purposes of protecting shareholders and ensuring that the firm operates efficiently within its political and cultural environment.

To summarize, the key theories employed by previous corporate governance studies are stewardship theory, agency theory, stakeholder theory and transaction cost theory. The first of these is inappropriate for a Libya-based study given the high incidence of nepotism when it comes to executive appointments; the widespread abuse of the appointment process means that many managers are neither qualified nor reliable. The second, agency theory, is also inappropriate for a developing country such as Libya, where the banking sector is characterized by concentrated state ownership and an underdeveloped capital market. What is more, the theory takes no account of the informal institutions that play a prominent role in Libyan corporate governance. Consequently, it is unlikely to clarify the behaviour of Libyan commercial banks in regard to corporate governance disclosure and practice. Stakeholder theory is relatively less developed and therefore unlikely to yield useful insights into how to improve corporate governance performance, while transaction cost theory has been accused of lacking generalizability and giving scant attention to the effect of context.

4.3 Institutional Theory

The economic theories discussed above were not selected as framework for analysis in the current study, as they were considered insufficient to interpret the development of corporate governance disclosure and practice within the institutional environment (Letza, Kirkbride, Sun and Smallman 2008). An alternative perspective was therefore needed (Learmount 2002). Institutional theory was selected as the theoretical lens for exploring corporate governance disclosures by Libyan banks, as prior research has paid little attention to the institutional environment surrounding LCBs. The theory is applied here to explain how Libya's institutional context has influenced/is influencing corporate governance disclosure and practice in the country's commercial banks.

Variations of institutional theory have been employed by scholars in a range of disciplines, including sociology, politics and economics (DiMaggio and Powell 1983; Moll, Burns and Major 2006; Scott 2001, 2008). These variations, which include old institutional economics (OIE), new institutional economics (NIE) and old and new institutional sociology (NIS) (Burns and Scapens 2000; Deegan and Unerman 2006; Moll, Burns and Major 2006) are discussed in the following sections.

4.3.1 The Development of Institutional Theory

4.3.1.1 Institutional Theory in Economics

Old institutional economics emerged 100 years ago (Moll, Burns and Major 2006). With the arguments that economic practices take place within a social context that is itself shaped by history and culture (Schmoller 1900), and that institutions are social phenomena that need theoretical explanation. Proponents of OIE criticized classical economic models for ignoring historical change and for their unrealistic assumptions about human behaviour. Veblen (1898) argued that this behaviour is largely governed by convention and habit., Veblen defined institutions as "settled habits of thought common to the generality of man" (Williamson 1996, p. 239). Commons, meanwhile, suggested that human behaviour is less suitable as a principle of economic analysis than transactions. He defined a transaction as "two or more wills giving, taking, persuading, coercing, defrauding, commanding, obeying, competing, governing, in a world of scarcity, mechanisms and rules of conduct" (Commons 1924, p.7).

4.3.1.2 Institutional Theory in Political Science

Institutional approaches influenced political science through the work of pioneers such as Wilson (1889), Willoughby (1896) and Burgess (1902). Between 1860 and 1925, these and other writers made moral philosophy and law the basis of their institutional analysis (Simon 1991). Their focus was on the administrative arrangements and legal frameworks which form governance constructions (Scott 2008). Bill and Hardgrave (1981) show that at the turn of the 20th century, institutional approaches focused on legal systems and formal structures, origins rather than change, historical reform and moral philosophy rather than empirical research. Between 1930 and 1960, however, the old institutional perspective faced increasing criticism from behaviourists keen to recast political science as an empirical as well as theoretical discipline (Scott 2008). The old institutional approach paid little attention to issues such as the informal distribution of power, political behaviour and attitudes (Hall and Thelen 2009), but under the influence of behaviourism, increasing consideration was given to topics such as public opinion, voting behaviour, party formation, action as a product of self-interest and allocation of resources (March and Olsen 1984). As a result of this revolution, a new variant of institutional theory emerged during the 1970s and 1980s, the aim of which was to reconstruct the frameworks that control, empower and constrain political behaviour.

4.3.1.3 Institutional Theory in Sociology

Spencer (1876, 1896, 1910) developed the concept of the institution with his description of society as an arrangement of "organs" or systems which over time develop into institutional structures. Sumner (1906) built on the work of Spencer by investigating the origin and development of "folkways". He argued that institutions are made up of concepts (which define the function or purpose of the institution) and structures (which put this function into action). Although the evolutionary view of institutions developed by Spencer and Sumner was subsequently rejected by sociologists, the concept had by then become established as a sociological focal point (Scott 2008).

Scott (2008) suggests that institutional analysis has been most influenced by Marx, Durkheim and Weber. Marx took a materialist view, regarding political and economic structures as the product of human ideas and actions. Durkheim (1893/1949) emphasized the role played by symbolic systems such as belief, knowledge, religion and morality, which he saw as social institutions, while Weber (1978) shed light on the cultural rules that describe social structures and govern social behaviour. According to Weber, the action is social where the researcher and object of study are characterized by the subjective meaning of events and the action itself is guided and motivated by material conditions and interests. This approach formed the basis of new institutional analysis (Scott 2008). Parsons (1934/1990) sought to resolve the tension between the subjective and objective approaches by arguing that normative frameworks emerge and exist independently of social actors (Scott 2008). He defined institutions as systems that regulate and organize the associations among people. However, Parsons' approach was challenged (Alexander 1983; Powell and DiMaggio 1991; Scott 2008) on the grounds that firstly, it gave more attention to cultural patterns than cognitive dimensions and secondly, his view of culture was limited to value orientations. The criticism left the way open for new institutional theory to find new and better ways to explain the relationship between the normative and the instrumental in social action.

New institutional sociology (NIS) is particularly suitable for the current study because it explains how organisational structures and practices are shaped by institutional pressure. NIS posits that the survival of an organisation depends not just on its achieving production efficiency but also on its conformity to social norms of acceptable practice (DiMaggio and Powell 1983; Meyer and Rowan 1977); in other words, on complying (or at least appearing to comply) with these institutional forces.

4.3.1.4 The Differences Between Old and New Institutionalism

According to Powell and DiMaggio, old and new institutionalism have a number of things in common:

> Both the old and new approaches share scepticism toward rational-actor models of organisation, and each views institutionalization as a state-dependent process that makes organisations less instrumentally rational by limiting the options they can pursue. Both emphasize the relationship between organisations and their environments, and both promise to reveal aspects of reality that are inconsistent with organisations' formal account. Each approach stresses the role of culture in shaping organisational reality. (Powell and DiMaggio 1991, p. 12)

However, there are also some significant differences:

> They identify different sources of constraint, with the older emphasizing the vesting of interests within organisations as a result of political trade-offs and alliances, and the new stressing the relationship between stability and legitimacy and the power of common understandings that are seldom explicitly articulated. (Powell and DiMaggio 1991, p.12)

Table 4.1: Differences Between Old and New Institutionalism.

	Old	New
Conflicts of interest	Central	Peripheral
Sources of inertia	Vested interests	Legitimacy imperative
Structural emphasis	Informal structure	Symbolic role of formal structure
Organisation embedded in	Local community	Field, sector, or society
Locus of institutionalisation	Organisation	Field of society
Organisation dynamics	Change	Persistence
Basis of critique of utilitarianism	Theory of interest aggregation	Theory of action
Evidence of critique of Utilitarianism	Unanticipated consequences	Unreflective activity
Key forms of cognition	Values, norms, attitudes	Classifications, routines, scripts, schema
Social psychology	Socialisation theory	Attribution theory
Cognitive basis of order	Commitment	Habit, practical action
Goals	Displaced	Ambiguous
Agenda	Policy relevance	Disciplinary

Source: Powell and DiMaggio (1991, p. 12).

The importance attributed to legitimacy is identified as a main difference between the two variants; in new institutional theory, this is seen as the key to organisational survival (Meyer and Rowan 1977). Table 4.1 summarizes how old and new institutionalism differ in their assumptions.

The following sections discuss those aspects of institutional theory that are most relevant to this study.

4.3.2 Institutional Isomorphism

DiMaggio and Powell argue that "[i]nstitutions become similar over time through the process of institutional isomorphism as organisations adapt to become increasingly similar to those around them. Isomorphism arises through three avenues: coercive, normative, and mimetic" (DiMaggio and Powell 1983, p. 150). Coercive isomorphism, they explain, "comes about as the result of external regulatory-type pressures for organisational convergence" (DiMaggio and Powell 1983, p. 150). These pressures mandate organisations to adopt a set of specific roles. They generally take the form of new codes or laws, followed by monitoring. Organisations violating the laws are punished while those demonstrating compliance are rewarded (DiMaggio and Powell 1983; Moll, Burns and Major 2006; Scott 1995). A prime example of coercive isomorphism within the Libyan banking sector is the CGLBS (2010), which obliges Libyan commercial banks to apply corporate governance best practice.

Mimetic isomorphism arises when organisations in the same field imitate each other's practice (DiMaggio and Powell 1983); those facing uncertainties tend to copy other successful organisations in the hope of enjoying similar success (Greenwood and Hinings 1996; Greenwood, Suddaby and Hinings 2002). This form of isomorphism is more likely to occur in smaller or less successful organisations and in those with ill-defined goals (DiMaggio and Powell 1983). Within the LBS, small banks are more likely to be encouraged to practise corporate governance disclosure if they see it being adopted by larger, successful institutions.

Finally, DiMaggio and Powell (1983) explain that normative isomorphism results when organisations feel under pressure to adhere to standards set by experts and professional bodies at national and international levels. Unlike coercive pressure, there is no legal or regulatory obligation to comply with these norms (Scott 1995), but the organisation may see it as necessary to maintain legitimacy within the sector.

However, as suggested in Section 4.3.1.3, this compliance may not always be genuine; many organisations choose to respond to institutional pressures by decoupling their actual practice from the formal requirements (Moll, Burns and Major 2006). This phenomenon has inspired numerous studies within NIS (Fiss and Zajac 2006, 2004; Wade, Porac and Pollock 1997; Westphal and Zajac 1994, 1998, 2001; Zajac and Westphal 1995). In terms of corporate governance specifically, Krenn (2014) explains that convergence is often merely formal rather than substantive, with some firms that have formally adopted a code of good governance decoupling this policy from their actual practice. He provides a model explaining the circumstances under which firms may pursue a decoupling strategy in response to conflicting pressures in their institutional environment, arguing that this tends to happen when: (a) the firm's compliance costs are relatively high, (b) the cost to the firm of outright and visible non-compliance is relatively high, and (c) outsiders' compliance monitoring costs are relatively high, (Krenn 2014, p. 110). Within the Libyan context, commercial banks tend to decouple their corporate governance from their actual practice and treat corporate governance disclosure as a formality rather than an intrinsically worthwhile task.

4.3.3 The Three Institutional Pillars

Scott describes institutions as comprising "regulative, normative and cultural-cognitive elements that, together with associated activities and resources provide stability and meaning to social life" (Scott 2008, p. 48). These three pillars of organisational legitimacy: regulative, normative and cultural-cognitive (see Table 4.2).

Table 4.2: The Three Institutional Pillars.

	Regulative	**Normative**	**Cultural-Cognitive**
Basis of compliance	Expedience	Social obligation	Taken-for-grantedness Shared understanding
Basis of order	Regulative rules	Binding expectations	Constitutive schema
Mechanisms	Coercive	Normative	Mimetic
Logic	Instrumentality	Appropriateness	Orthodoxy
Indicators	Rules Laws Sanctions	Certification Accreditation	Common beliefs Shared logics of Action Isomorphism
Basis of legitimacy	Legally sanctioned	Morally governed	Comprehensible Recognizable Culturally supported

Source: Scott (2008, p. 51).

Scott gives more attention to the context where the organisation is working rather than creating change and homogenizing companies in specific organisational fields. He provides three pillars which can create the context of the stability of the organisation through its structures and activities. This definition is wide and has a variety of themes which will be discussed in the following sections. These three institutional pillars may be used to explain the institutionalization process.

4.3.3.1 Regulative Pillar

The regulative pillar has been discussed widely by institutional researchers (Scott 2008). It contains regulatory processes (rule-setting, monitoring and sanctioning activities) the purpose of which is to shape future behaviour. The legal framework controls companies by force, applying sanctions against those who deviate from the rules (it should be noted that these rules may reflect the interests of those who make them). The sanctions are grounded in instrumental logic, driving companies to behave legitimately in order to avoid penalties (Hoffman 1999). This may involve them applying new pollution-control technologies to adhere to environmental rules, for example, or hiring accountants to comply with tax law requirements (DiMaggio and Powell 1983).

In Libya, the CGLBS (2010) requires Libyan commercial banks to follow corporate governance principles; as discussed in Section 3.4, the code is one of a number of reforms designed to force banks to follow best corporate governance practice. Scott (2008) explains that each regulative pillar is carried through certain key institutional carriers; in the case of the CGLBS (2010), the code carries procedures for the practice and disclosure of corporate governance, allowing principals to monitor agents and assess their compliance with set legal protocols. The code was designed to improve the level of corporate governance disclosure in the LBS. The current research.

4.3.3.2 Normative Pillar

The normative pillar includes two elements: values serve as a measure of existing and ideal practice, while norms provide a guiding principle for how this practice should be achieved (Gibbs 1965). According to Scott, the normative pillar involves "the creation of expectations that introduce a prescriptive, evaluative, and obligatory dimension into social life" (Scott 2008, p. 880). Organisations feel obliged to adhere to these expectations, whether they are general societal beliefs or the norms set by trade bodies, to preserve legitimacy (Hoffman 1999).

In the Libyan context, banks may be influenced by international organisations such as the BCSB, OECD and the Basel Committee to adopt corporate governance guidelines. These organisations expect banks to comply with international corporate governance principles and practices. At the national level, the LSM expects listed banks to comply with its voluntary corporate governance code, while organisations such as the Libyan Accountants and Auditors' Association (LAAA) and the Libyan Audit Bureau expect banks to adhere to both national and international standard requirements.

4.3.3.3 Cultural-cognitive Pillar

The cultural-cognitive pillar refers to the shared beliefs and culture that underlie organisations' mimetic behaviour. These beliefs are usually grounded in an established orthodoxy or commonly accepted understanding of how things are done. As mentioned in Section 4.3.2, organisations often respond to uncertainty in the external environment by engaging in mimetic behaviour (DiMaggio and Powell 1983) that affirms their acceptance of and adherence to this orthodoxy; as Scott explains: "[M] imetic isomorphism is driven by the constitutive schemas or the way things have been done" (Scott 2008, p. 51). The cultural-cognitive pillar contains carriers which are the symbolic representation of the internal environment. In the LBS, organisational attributes such as age and ownership structure carry symbolic significance and have an impact on the development of corporate governance disclosure and practice.

4.3.4 Institutional Fields

An institutional field may be defined as "those organisations that in the aggregate, constitute a recognised area of institutional life: key suppliers, resources and product consumers, regulatory agencies and other organisations that produce similar services and see themselves involved in a common enterprise" (DiMaggio and

Powell 1983, p. 143). By this definition, the institutional field of the Libyan banking sector includes all commercial banks, regulators and legislators.

However, Scott's (1995) suggestion that organisations participate in a system of common meaning as they see themselves as a part of a community implies that the definition may be expanded to encompass all those who share this common meaning system and who interact with each other more than with outside actors.

Analysing the institutional field thus requires the researcher to take into account not only the role played by the main actors but also that played by other stakeholders such as the state, regulators, professional and trade associations and product consumers (DiMaggio and Powell 1983), all of whom have their own agendas (Everett 2002). In the case of LCBs, related actors also include foreign investors, though the main actor remains the CBL, which has part-ownership in the majority of commercial banks.

4.3.5 New Institutional Theory and The Concept of Institutional Logics

A review of the literature suggests that the main focus of institutional theory is how and why organisations in the same field become more or less homogeneous over time (Scott 2008). Researchers have identified many reasons why organisations change, but a recurring explanation is that they do so in response to changes in the institutional field. Hoffman and Wooten (2008), for example, indicate that the arrival of new competitors within the field increases institutional pressures, forcing organisations to respond, while Greenwood, Suddaby and Hinings (2002) point to the impact of technological and regulatory changes.

Recent developments in institutional theory include Scott's (2008) broadened view of institutional theory as a discipline or meta-theory dealing with organisations and institutions (i.e. the taken-for-granted ways of organizing), the institutional lifecycle (i.e. the rise and fall of institutions), institutional change and stability (i.e. prevention of change) and organisational resistance to institutions (i.e. symbolic and illegitimate action).

Fiss (2008) points to corporate governance as an example of how institutions impact social phenomena. He notes that while the ideological battle continues over whether shareholders or stakeholders should have primacy, the shareholder-oriented model remains dominant. Fiss (2008) also highlights resistance to the shareholder value maximisation model of corporate governance despite its diffusion. He highlights the preferences and relative power of companies and their stakeholders, particularly shareholders and directors, as a function of diffusion. He argues that mimetic isomorphism is not the cause of diffusion as companies adhere to local requirements, although their adaptation may be impacted by cultural, political and technical concerns. Fiss points to decoupling and efforts to change societal expectations as a form of company resistance. He also suggests that there are several interests for shareholders such that the corporate objective cannot be the only shareholder-oriented as argued by its supporters. Finally, he suggests that the fact that capitalism takes different forms around the world is related to the variation in corporate governance frameworks. However, institutional pressure may transfer globally and lead to diffuse a global conjunction in corporate governance.

Another development is the emergence of the concept of institutional logic. Dunn and Jones define institutional logics as "cultural beliefs and rules that shape the cognitions and behaviours of actors" (Dunn and Jones 2010, p. 114). They are "socially shared, deeply held assumptions and values that form a framework for reasoning, provide criteria for legitimacy, and help organize time and space" (Dunn and Jones 2010, p. 114). Institutional logics help make social reality clear and guide individuals' actions (Friedland and Alford 1991; Thornton and Ocasio 1999), but as socially-constructed sets of ideas, they may contain inconsistencies or uncertainties (van Gestel and Hillebrand 2011). From organisational subsystems to world-systems , institutional logics exist at multiple levels, often in competition (Friedland and Alford 1991). This competition and uncertainty can leave the way open for certain organisational actors to impose on others ideas or practices that serve their own interests (Seo and Creed 2002; Suddaby and Greenwood 2005), giving them the power to play a central role in organisational change (Thornton and Ocasio 2008; Suddaby and Greenwood 2005).

There have been numerous changes in the LBS – both regulatory and otherwise – since 2005, including the issuing of the Libyan Banking Law in 2005, the voluntary CGLBS in 2006, the establishment of the LSM in 2007, the entry of foreign banks and the issuing of the mandatory CGLBS in 2010 and the seismic cultural and political shifts since the revolution of 2011. All of these changes may have affected the development of corporate governance and disclosure in Libya and assisted in differentiating it from corporate governance in other developing and developed countries. The CBL's role as a majority shareowner in a number of LCBs (see Table 3.2) means it should have a major influence on corporate governance disclosure in the sector, but this is offset by a weak monitoring environment. Libya's shift from socialism to capitalism, and the accompanying change in social and political culture, have also had an impact, with reforms to liberalize the economy creating an institutional logic which must now compete with the logic that prevailed under the former regime. Institutional pressure is thus relatively weak, leaving many organisations free to decouple their activities from the legal requirements of the CGLBS (2010).

4.3.6 Institutions

Scholars have defined the concept of the institution from different perspectives, depending on their approach to institutional theory. Stinchcombe, for example, defines it from the power perspective, describing an institution as "a structure in which powerful people are committed to some value or interest" (Stinchcombe 1968, p. 107). Jepperson, meanwhile, focuses on the exercise of power, describing institutions as patterns of social practice in which "departures from the pattern are counteracted in a regulated fashion, by repetitively activated, socially constructed, controls – that is by some set of rewards and sanctions" (Jepperson 1991, p. 145). In focusing on the acquisition and exercise of power, both definitions echo the main concern of corporate governance. Other researchers define the concept from the perspective of inter-personal relationships. Thus, Barley and Tolbert define institutions as "shared rules and typifications that identify categories of social actors and their appropriate activities or relationships" (Barley and Tolbert 1997, p. 96). Burns and Scapens extend this definition, describing institutions as "the shared, taken-for -granted assumptions which identify categories of human actors and their appropriate activities and relationships" (Burns and Scapens 2000, p. 8). Other scholars define institutions from an even wider perspective; Huntington (1968), for example, describes them as governance structures made up of cultural elements (e.g. rules, norms, values, roles, systems, behaviours and formal and informal procedures) that form and define the relationships between individuals within the institution and between the institution and the prevailing political, economic and social systems. Adopting a similarly broad view, Khadaroo and Shaikh (2007) asserts that an institution may be made up of a variety of organisations connected by a shared aim, such as achieving corporate governance best practice.

The literature highlights the key role played by institutions such as the bureaucratic state, religion, the market, the law, politics, and kinship and family.

4.3.6.1 The Bureaucratic State

Watson (2007) emphasizes that all organisations are subject to the authority of the bureaucratic state, or as Weber (1978) puts it, legitimized power plays a central role in organisational practice. Greenwood, Raynard, Kodeih, Micelotta, Lounsbury identify two ways of state logic: "Relative tolerance is shown towards political representation and plurality of expression and the extent to which state powers and authority are centrally concentrated or devolved to sub-national levels" (Greenwood, Raynard, Kodeih, Micelotta, and Lounsbury 2011, p. 573). Regarding state logic, democratic participation is the basis of legitimacy, bureaucratic domination is the basis of authority, social and economic context is the basis of identity and the source of strategy is to improve the community and make it better (Thornton, Ocasio and Lounsbury 2012). The bureaucratization process varies from one society to another, with variation in bureaucracy appearing clearly when organisations are rationalized or modernized (Watson and Korczynski 2011). The bureaucratic state can have a supportive or discouraging impact on organisational practice. Bourdieu and Farage explain that some issues such as educational failure, poverty and immigration are characteristics through societies. He also states that "[s]tate bureaucracies and their representatives are great producers of 'social problems' [and] social science does little more than ratify whenever it takes them over as 'sociological' problems" (Bourdieu and Farage 1994, p. 2).

There is little in the literature regarding the impact of the bureaucratic state on the emergence and development of corporate governance. Che and Qian (1998) argue that as local regulatory authorities derive their power from the state, they have the potential to play a key role in improving society. In terms of corporate governance, this means on the one hand supporting companies by offering training and consultation, and on the other enforcing the rules and applying penalties where necessary. However, as Becht, Bolton and Roell (2003) observe, the rules imposed by these authorities may be inadequate or inconsistently enforced.

As the main regulatory body in the Libyan banking sector, the CBL has been tasked with implementing corporate governance in Libyan commercial banks. To this end, it issued the CGLBS (2010), which requires banks to disclose not just their financial information but also information about their organisational structure, corporate governance practice and structure and ethical standards. However, there has been no investigation of the CBL's role in supporting and enforcing the implementation of this code; Zagoub (2011) makes a start by identifying coercive institutional pressure from the CBL as the biggest determinant of LCBs' corporate governance practice, but he points to the need for further research into the varying levels of compliance demonstrated by both listed and unlisted banks.

4.3.6.2 Religion

Religion plays a central role in many people's worldview as a source of explanation and even prediction (Davie 2006). According to Asad, "There cannot be a universal definition of religion, not only because its constituent elements and relationships are historically specific, but because that definition is itself the historical product of discursive processes" (Asad 2009, p. 29). However, Friedland and Alford (1991) argue that at the heart of all major religions is the search for transcendental truth; this forms the core of their institutional logic, informing their norms and values to varying degrees. To those impacted by religion, faith and sacredness are sources of legitimacy, religious scholars are sources of authority and God is the source of identity (Thornton, Ocasio and Lounsbury 2012). From a sociological perspective, religion is widely perceived as the main component of an integrative value system (Parsons 1991). The literature suggests that religion impacts on corporate governance in some societies; Abu-tapanjeh (2009), for example, indicates that religious teachings encouraging adherence to principles such as justice, honesty and public spiritedness also play an important part in protecting shareholders and promoting good corporate governance practice. Indeed, Abu-tapanjeh argues that an ethical/moral structure is essential in any governance system as without it, the system will fail. Rizk (2008) also points to the key role religion plays in encouraging ethical behaviour. In the Libyan context, the dominant religion is Islam and as such, it plays an important role in Libyan society (see Section 3.2.3).

4.3.6.3 Kinship and Family

Radcliffe-Brown defines the institution of kinship as "a system of dyadic relations between person and person in a community, the behaviour of any two persons in any of these relations being regulated in some way, and to a greater or less extent, by social usage" (Radcliffe-Brown 1941, p. 2). The kinship institution has been widely discussed in the literature, which sees it as playing an important social role. Young and Wilmott state that "[k]inship remains an important force in most people's lives, and is in particular still overwhelmingly the main source of informal care and support" (Young and Wilmott 2013, p. xxiii). From a corporate governance perspective, the literature notes that kinship has an impact on corporate governance, particularly in developing countries (Young, Peng, Ahlstrom, Bruton and Jiang 2008). This impact manifests in a number of ways, such as reduced board independence, an increase in corruption and a culture of secrecy. The first of these is highlighted by Bukhari (2014), who, in his investigation of the impact of a range of institutions on corporate governance in Saudi Arabian listed companies, found that kinship ties undermine the independence of board members. The effect of this loss of independence is illustrated by Filatotchev, Lien and Piesse (2005) when they investigated the impact on board performance of ownership structure and board characteristics in listed, family-owned companies in developing countries, they found that boards dominated by family members tended to perform less well.

Kinship's effect on company openness has also been demonstrated by researchers, with Qu and Leung (2006) finding that Chinese society's clan-oriented culture deters Chinese listed companies from providing comprehensive corporate governance information, and Arafa (2012) linking the culture of secrecy among family-owned Egyptian companies to their lack of online disclosure. The increased incidence of corruption has been illustrated by Dela Rama (2012), who found that in the Philippines, where family-owned business groups dominate, corruption has had a significant impact on the development of corporate governance. As Section 3.2.4 reveals, the extended family is the cornerstone of Libyan society, shaping the structure of contemporary life.

4.3.6.4 The Market

Different theoretical schools have discussed markets as institutions from a variety of perspectives. To neo-classical economists, the market institution is the backbone of the economy (Chang 2002), while the state serves as an alternative non-market institution (Aoki 1996). The market plays a central role in developed societies such as the US and UK as it creates stability and provides a social explanation for competition (Fligstein 1996; Fligstein and Mara-Drita 1996). In these societies, the institution of the market dominates because it is effective. However, it may be less effective in developing economies, which tend to be less well regulated (La Porta, Lopez-de-Silanes, Shleifer and Vishny 2000). Thornton, Ocasio and Lounsbury (2012) argue that market logic is grounded in self-interest and mainly concerned with economic value and profit-seeking; actors aim to improve market position by making cost efficiencies and/or increasing revenue. Since markets in developing countries tend to be weak, they are less effective at modifying this behaviour and driving organisations to implement corporate governance (Lin 2001). Allen (2005) goes further, citing China as an example of a developing country where the market has had virtually no impact on corporate governance. This study seeks to investigate the extent to which the market is impacting the development of corporate governance in Libya.

4.3.6.5 Political Institution

March and Olsen (1989) define the political institution as

> collections of interrelated rules and routines that define appropriate actions in terms of relations between roles and situations. The process involves determining what the situation is, what role is being fulfilled, and what the obligation of that role in that situation is.
>
> (March and Olsen 1989, p. 21)

The political institution encompasses the legal system, legislature, political parties, bureaucracies and mass media that collectively create the rules and govern the ownership and practice of political rights and resources (March and Olsen 1996). Watts (1977) sees the political process as essentially a competition in which each participant is seeking to maximize their own interests. If this is the case, the agency relationship may be seen on one level as reflective of the political process.

Few studies have investigated the impact of political institutions on corporate governance, and most of these were conducted in developed countries, but in one of these studies, Roe concludes that "[p]olitics can press managers to stabilise employment, to forego some profit-maximising risks with the firm, and to use up capital in place rather than to downsize when markets are no longer aligned with the firm's production capabilities" (Roe 2003, p. iii). Watts (1977) argues that political parties can play an essential role in demanding and regulating financial disclosure from corporations, and points out that issuing disclosure-related regulations represents one means by which governments have historically responded to political crises. The UK government responded to the South Sea Bubble crisis by issuing the Parliament Act of 1720 forbidding the establishment of joint-stock companies, while the US Government's Securities Acts of 1933 and 1934 were a response to the US stock market crash in 1929. Political parties can also choose to respond (or not) to the actions of lobbyists.

In the Libyan context, the former regime's political ideology played the main role in shaping the national economy.

4.3.6.6 The Law

The literature discusses the legal institution from two main perspectives: the law as an exploration of power, or as the source of, or need for, power (La Torre 2010). Weinberger (1991) builds on the institutional theory of law, observing that norms exist as "thought objects" and belong to the "institutional facts" of our social existence. A growing body of literature is addressing the impact of the legal institution on the development of corporate governance. According to Milhaupt (1996), the law plays an important role in shaping corporate governance in developed countries, setting out the basic principle of corporate governance, describing the rights of actors and setting the limits for private ordering. Shleifer and Vishny (1997) point particularly to the institution's role in protecting investors and shareholders, while Cioffi (2000) adds that company law, financial market regulation and labour law all have an impact on companies' corporate governance. Although this may be the case in developed countries, in developing countries, the legal environment often seems inconsistent with the development of corporate governance. Young, Peng, Ahlstrom, Bruton and Jiang (2008) indicate that although many developing countries have adopted the Anglo-American system of corporate governance, many elements of the legal institution, such as disclosure parameters, accounting requirements and securities trading boundaries, are inadequate or absent altogether. In these circumstances, it is highly likely that corporate governance will be driven by other institutions such as kinship ties, government connections and business groups (Yeung 2006).

4.4 Summary

The first part of this chapter describes and evaluates the theories commonly used by researchers to investigate corporate governance and disclosure. It starts with stewardship theory, which sees executives as stewards who are motivated to work in the best interests of shareholders (Davis, Schoorman and Donaldson 1997; Donaldson and Davis 1991). Critics of this theory point to the role played by executive opportunism in numerous corporate collapses. In contrast to the optimistic view taken by stewardship theory, agency theory sees people as essentially self-interested; it posits that as a result, any cooperative action is likely to produce conflicts of interest (Jensen, 1994; Agrawal and Knoeber 1996). Although useful, agency theory does not consider the impact of historical and cultural background or institutional arrangements on the agent-principal relationship. Stakeholder theory offers a broader perspective, focusing not just on shareholders but also customers, suppliers, employees, government, auditors and the wider community (Letza, Sun and Kirkbride, 2004), but it has been criticized as insufficiently developed for investigating corporate governance (Sternberg, 1997). Transaction cost theory, which assumes that companies get larger and more complex as a result of the price changes outside companies which guide the production and the markets coordinate transaction (Solomon, 2013), has also been criticized – for lacking generalizability and paying too little attention to context.

The second half of the chapter discusses the institutional theory framework. It explains that institutional theory has given rise to several variations, including old institutional economics (OIE), new institutional economics (NIE) and new institutional sociology (NIS) (Burns and Scapens 2000; Deegan and Unerman 2006; Moll, Burns and Major 2006). The chapter discusses the concept of institutional isomorphism introduced by DiMaggio and Powell (1983) and Scott's (2008) three institutional pillars. before going on to discuss the concepts of institutional fields and institutional logics. Finally, it introduces those key institutions (the bureaucratic state, religion, kinship, the market, politics and the law) that have been identified in the literature as having an impact on corporate governance.

5 Analysis of Annual Reports and Websites of LCBs

5.1 Introduction

This chapter presents and analyses the data that were gathered from the annual reports and websites published by the sixteen commercial banks in Libya.

The chapter comprises four sections: the first (5.2) presents and analyses the descriptive information and statistics relating to corporate governance disclosure for the sample as a whole (sixteen banks). The second section (5.3) considers how corporate governance disclosure varies between the banks. The third section (5.4) compares corporate governance disclosure performance of LCBs with that of companies in other developing countries. Finally, the fourth section (5.5) traces the development of corporate governance disclosure in eleven of the sixteen commercial banks, as revealed in their annual reports and websites over the last ten years.

5.2 Descriptive Analysis of the Overall Extent of Corporate Governance Disclosure

This section provides a descriptive analysis of the banks' corporate governance disclosure practice, as revealed in their annual reports and websites (see Table 5.1 for the recent years covered by these annual reports and websites). It is divided into two sub-sections: Section 6.2.1 discusses the overall extent of corporate governance disclosure across the sixteen banks; Section 6.2.2 presents the descriptive statistics for corporate governance disclosure by information category.

5.2.1 Overall Extent of Corporate Governance Disclosure Across the Sixteen Banks

Corporate governance disclosure practice in the sample banks was measured using UNCTAD's ISAR international benchmark. This comprises a list of 52 specific corporate governance disclosure items, grouped into five categories. Table 5.1 presents an overview of the number of banks in the sample publishing information on each of the ISAR corporate governance disclosure items. The table shows that the highest level of disclosure was in the area of financial transparency, with an average of 5.25 banks disclosing information on one or more items in this group. The lowest level of disclosure (average 0) was found in the group of items relating to auditing. None of the items was disclosed by all sixteen banks, and only one (financial and operating results) was disclosed by fifteen. Seven disclosure items were disclosed by eight or more banks. Among

https://doi.org/10.1515/9783110602111-005

Table 5.1: Compliance with The ISAR Benchmark Across The Sample as a Whole.

Ownership structure and exercise of control rights	**Number of banks disclosing item (n = 16)**
Changes in shareholdings*	8
Control and corresponding equity stake	0
Control rights	0
Ownership structure*	12
Process for holding annual general meetings	1
Availability and accessibility of meeting agenda	0
Control structure	0
Rules and procedures governing the acquisition of corporate control in capital markets	0
Anti-takeover measures	0
Average	**2.33**
Financial transparency	
Financial and operating results*	15
Board's responsibilities regarding financial communications	1
Company objectives*	14
Nature, type and elements of related party transactions*	0
The decision-making process for approving transactions with related parties	0
Rules and procedures governing extraordinary transactions	0
Critical accounting estimates	12
Impact of alternative accounting decisions	0
Average	**5.25**
Auditing	
Process for appointment of external auditors	0
Internal control systems	0
Process for interaction with external auditors	0
Process for appointment of internal auditors/Scope of work and responsibilities	0
Process for interaction with internal auditors	0
Board confidence in independence and integrity of external auditors	0
Auditors' involvement in non-audit work and the fees paid to auditors	0
Duration of current auditors	0
Rotation of audit partners	0
Average	**0**
Board and management structure and process	
Composition of board of directors (executives and non-executives)*	1

Table 5.1 (continued)

Ownership structure and exercise of control rights	**Number of banks disclosing item (n = 16)**
Governance structures, such as committees and other mechanisms to prevent conflicts of interest*	8
Role and functions of the board of directors*	0
Determination and composition of directors' remuneration*	1
Material interests of members of the board and management*	0
Composition and function of governance committee structures*	0
Qualifications and biographical information on board members*	3
"Checks and balances" mechanisms	0
Duration of directors' contracts	0
Independence of the board of directors*	0
Risk management objectives, system and activities*	5
Existence of plan of succession	0
Number of outside board and management position directorships held by directors*	0
Existence of procedure(s) for addressing conflicts of interest among board members	0
Types and duties of outside board and management positions*	0
Professional development and training activities	0
Availability and use of advisorship facility during reporting	0
Performance evaluation process	0
Compensation policy for senior executives departing the firm as a result of a merger or acquisition	0
Average	**0.94**
Corporate responsibility and compliance	
Mechanisms protecting the rights of other stakeholders in business	1
Policy and performance in connection with environmental and social responsibility*	11
A code of ethics for the board and waivers to the ethics code	0
A code of ethics for all company employees	0
The role of employees in corporate governance	0
Impact of environmental and social responsibility policies on the firm's sustainability	0
Policy on "whistleblower" protection for all employees	0
Average	**1.71**

*Legal requirement

these seven items, two were in the ownership structure and exercise of control rights group, three were in the financial transparency group, one was in the board and management structure and process group and one was in the corporate responsibility and compliance group.

Fourteen out of the 52 items in the ISAR benchmark were disclosed by at least one bank in the sample, while the other 38 items did not feature at all in the banks' reporting. These 38 include five items that are legally required: the nature, type and elements of related party transactions; material interests of members of the board and management; a code of ethics for all company employees; the role and functions of the board of directors; and the independence of the board of directors.

5.2.2 Descriptive Statistics for Corporate Governance Disclosure by Information Category

Having reviewed the results for the sample as a whole in the previous section, this section breaks down the findings and presents them by information category.

5.2.2.1 Ownership Structure and Exercise of Control Rights

The disclosure of information about ownership structure is essential if banks are to encourage investment. According to UNCTAD

> [t]he beneficiary ownership structure of an enterprise is of great importance in an investment decision, especially with regard to the equitable treatment of shareholders. In order to make an informed decision about the company, investors need access to information regarding its ownership structure. (UNCTAD 2006, p. 8)

The ownership structure and exercise of control rights category in the ISAR benchmark contains nine items. Companies aiming for good corporate governance disclosure practice should disclose information for all these items, but as Figure 5.1 shows, only three of the nine items were disclosed by the sample banks in their reports or websites. The majority (twelve) of the banks disclosed information about ownership structure, one half (eight) disclosed information about changes in shareholding, and just one disclosed information about the process for holding annual general meetings. The level of disclosure within the first two items varied, with some providing brief information about shareholder structure and others disclosing more details (examples and analysis for the different banks are provided in Section 5.5).

Only one bank disclosed information about the process for holding annual general meetings (AGMs) and no bank disclosed information regarding the availability or accessibility of meeting agenda. The procedures and rules for AGMs are

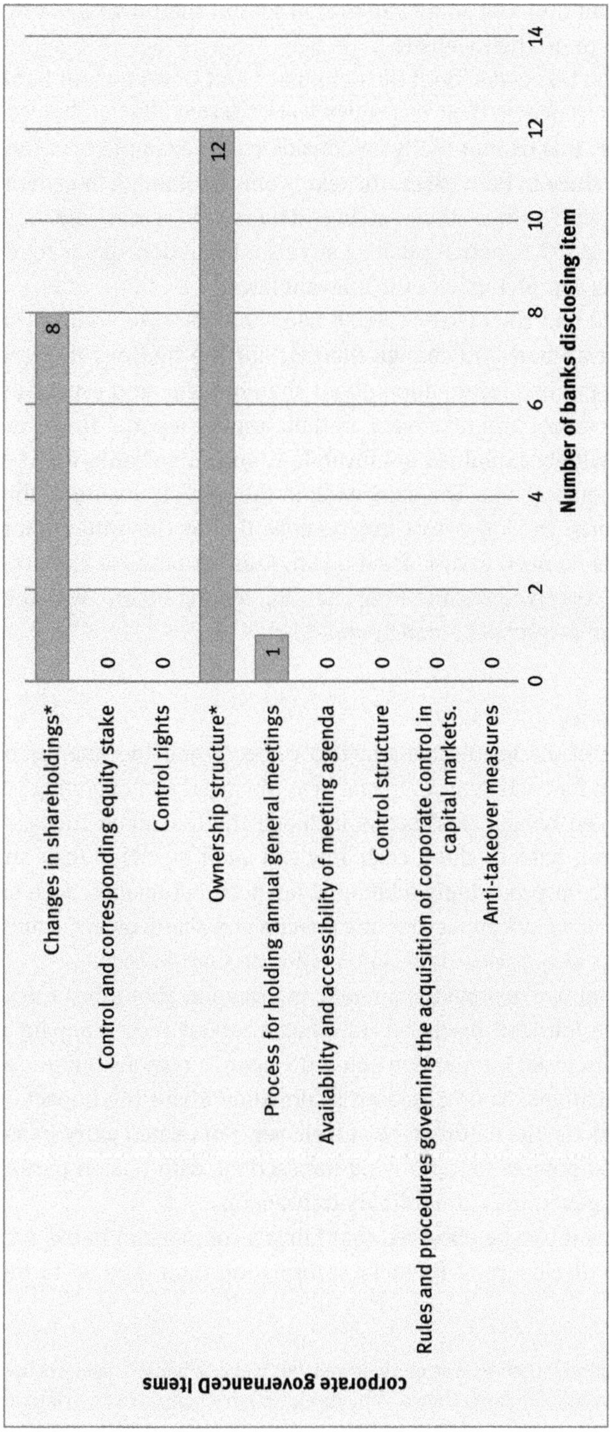

Figure 5.1: Ownership Structure and Exercise of Control Rights.

explained in detail in Libyan law, but some banks also set out their own AGM bylaws in their annual report or on their website.[1]

In relation to the item on takeovers, both the Commerce and Development Bank and Wahada Bank offer assurance on their respective websites that all shareholders have equal rights. However, this cannot really be considered an example of corporate governance disclosure since in both cases, the text is only explaining in general terms what should happen, rather than giving details of actual practice. Stakeholders are more interested in actual practice as this information serves to reassure them that the bank is complying with the relevant laws.

Under the CGLBS (2010) and the CGLSM (2007), banks are required to disclose details of ownership structure and any change therein, but the findings indicate that LCBs do not generally publish information about shareholders, and especially not information related to control and takeovers, in their annual reports. However, this kind of information is widely explained in Libyan law, and some banks also set out their own bylaws on their website. This may explain the non-disclosure of this information in annual reports; the key actors may assume that as this information is already available, there is no need to disclose it again. Another possible explanation is the lack of any real coercive pressure from the CBL, among others, which is itself attributable to a lack of awareness among regulators.

5.2.2.2 Financial Transparency

Figure 5.2 shows the range of disclosure items in this category and the number of banks proffering information for each item. Only one item (financial and operating results) was disclosed by fifteen banks. Most banks included the four main financial documents (income statement, balance sheet, cash flow and audit report) in their annual report, with the majority also providing additional financial information such as the CEO's statement, details of significant accounting policies and shareholders' equity statement. Some of the banks also disclosed this information on their website.

Twelve of the commercial banks provided numeric information about the critical accounting estimates, while fourteen disclosed information about their company's objectives. Only one bank disclosed information about the board's responsibilities regarding financial communications. None disclosed information about the impact of alternative accounting decisions, the nature, type and elements of related party transactions, the decision-making process for approving transactions with related parties or the rules and procedures governing extraordinary transactions.

From the above analysis it can be observed that Libya's commercial banks pay far greater attention to the disclosure of financial information than they do to the

1 Three out of sixteen banks disclosed their bylaws on their website: Wahada Bank, Commerce and Development Bank and Al-Ejmaa Alarabi Bank. United Bank discloses any changes to its bylaws in the general meeting.

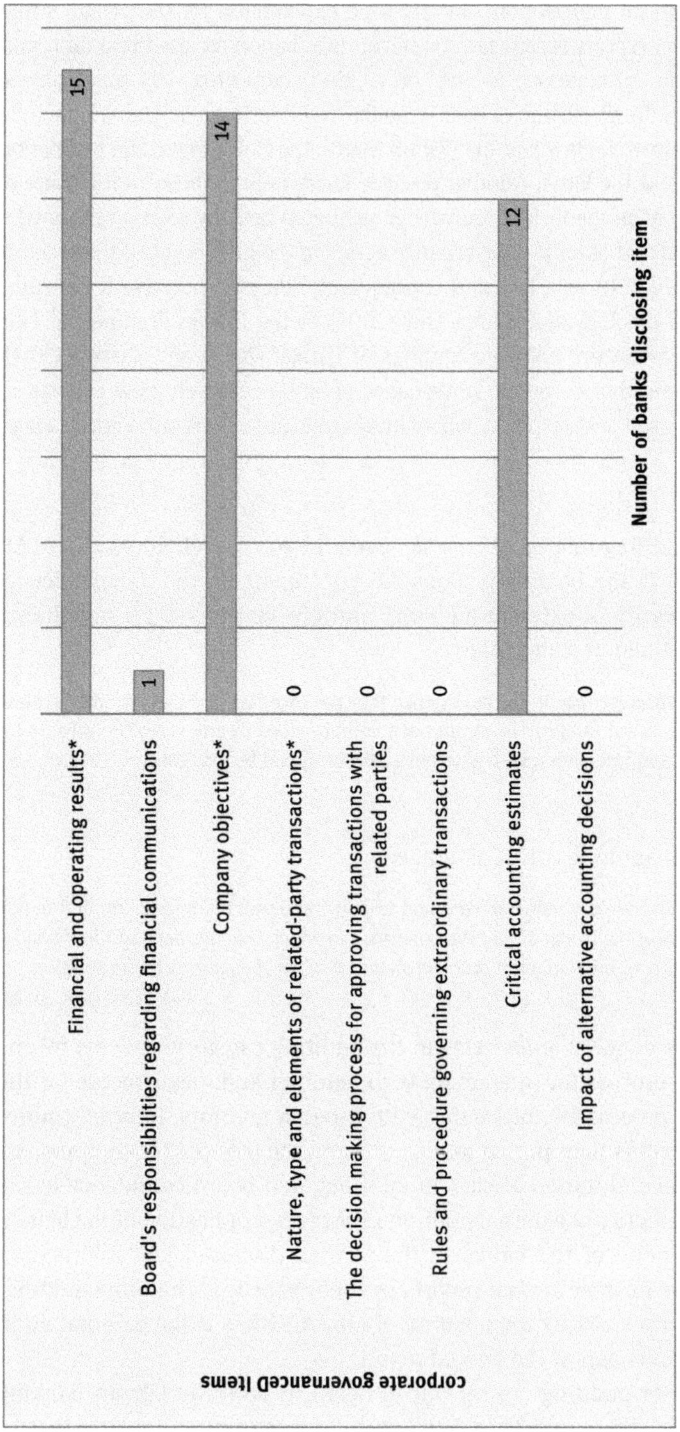

Figure 5.2: Financial Transparency.

disclosure of non-financial information. One possible explanation for this result is that those preparing annual reports regard non-financial information as less important, particularly as financial information is the only kind requested by stakeholders. Furthermore, although the disclosure of both financial and non-financial items is mandatory under Libyan commercial law and the CGLBS (2010), the CBL shows little inclination to force banks to disclose the latter. Another possible factor behind the non-disclosure of non-financial items may be the lack of knowledge exhibited both by some of those who prepare annual reports and other key governance actors in the LBS. Some of these actors do not see the CGLBS (2010) as a law and consequently, they do not give it the same attention they give to the Libyan Banking Law (2005) or the Libyan Commercial Law (2010). This result is consistent with the findings of Larbsh (2010) and Zagoub (2011), both of whom conclude that corporate governance is still a relatively new concept in Libya and that there is still a widespread lack of knowledge about corporate governance.

5.2.2.3 Auditing

The reporting of auditing-related issues is essential for stakeholders. UNCTAD (2006) asserts that it is the board's responsibility to report on the independence, competency and integrity of external auditors, and on the process for appointing and interacting with them. It states that:

> [t]he board should disclose that it has confidence that the external auditors are independent and their competency and integrity have not been compromised in any way. The process for the appointment of and interaction with external auditors should be disclosed.
>
> (UNCTAD 2006, p. 25)

In relation to internal auditing, UNCTAD states:

> Enterprises should disclose the scope of work and responsibilities of the internal audit function and the highest level of the leadership of the enterprise to which the internal audit function reports. Enterprises with no internal audit function should disclose the reasons for its absence.
>
> (UNCTAD 2006, p. 26)

The ISAR benchmark contains nine items in the auditing category: process for the appointment of and process for interacting with external auditors, process for the appointment of and process for interacting with internal auditors, internal control systems, auditors' involvement in non-audit work and the fees paid to auditors, rotation of audit partners, duration of current auditors, and board confidence in the independence and integrity of external auditors. However, application of the benchmark revealed that none of the banks in the sample disclosed any information about auditing either in their annual reports or their websites. The only auditing-related information disclosed by the majority of Libyan banks is the external auditors' report, which forms part of the annual report.

The procedures for auditing are set out in detail in both the Libyan Banking Law (2005) and the CGLBS (2010). The CGLBS (2010), for example, stipulates that

> [t]he bank must ensure that the external auditor audits the internal auditing system for the reports and financial disclosure; it must ensure that the external auditor is aware of the importance of their task and that this is done professionally. If possible, it should determine the scope of the auditing operation. All external and internal auditing tasks are the responsibility of the audit committee.
>
> The audit committee is responsible for appointing and dismissing external auditors, assessing the auditing operation, meeting with auditors and discussing their report with them, giving permission for any additional work the auditors consider necessary and protecting their independence. (CGLBS 2010, p. 29)

However, there is no explicit provision within the Libyan Banking Law (2005) requiring banks to disclose information about auditing issues, and the CGLBS (2010) requires only that banks provide a copy of all committee reports including those produced by the audit committee to the CBL. This cannot be considered genuine corporate governance disclosure as these reports are not made available to the public. The lack of disclosure requirements may be contributing significantly to the low level of auditing-related disclosure among commercial banks in Libya.

5.2.2.4 Board and Management Structure and Process

Figure 5.3 shows that eight banks disclosed information about the governance structures, such as committees and other mechanisms, that they have put in place to prevent conflicts of interest. Three banks out of sixteen disclosed information about the qualifications and biographical information of board members, whilst five disclosed details of their risk management objectives, system and activities. Two items the composition of the board of directors (executives and non-executives) and the determination and composition of directors' remuneration – were each disclosed by only one bank. None of the banks in the sample disclosed anything regarding the number of outside board and management positions held by directors, the role and function of the board, the duration of directors' contracts, succession plans, board independence or the existence of procedure(s) for addressing conflicts of interest among board members.

Overall, it can be concluded that although most of the items in this category are required under the CGLBS (2010), LCBs are poor at disclosing information about their boards and managers. There are several possible reasons for this, such as the lack of enforcement by the CBL and the recent change in culture. This change in culture, along with the instability that has afflicted Libya since 2011, may have had a negative impact upon the sector's attempts to improve disclosure and the preparation of annual reports.

5.2.2.5 Corporate Responsibility and Compliance

The concept of corporate responsibility is relatively new in Libya and as a result, most LCBs do not disclose information about it. The banks in the sample disclosed information for just two items in this category: just one bank gave information about its mechanisms for protecting the rights of other stakeholders, whereas

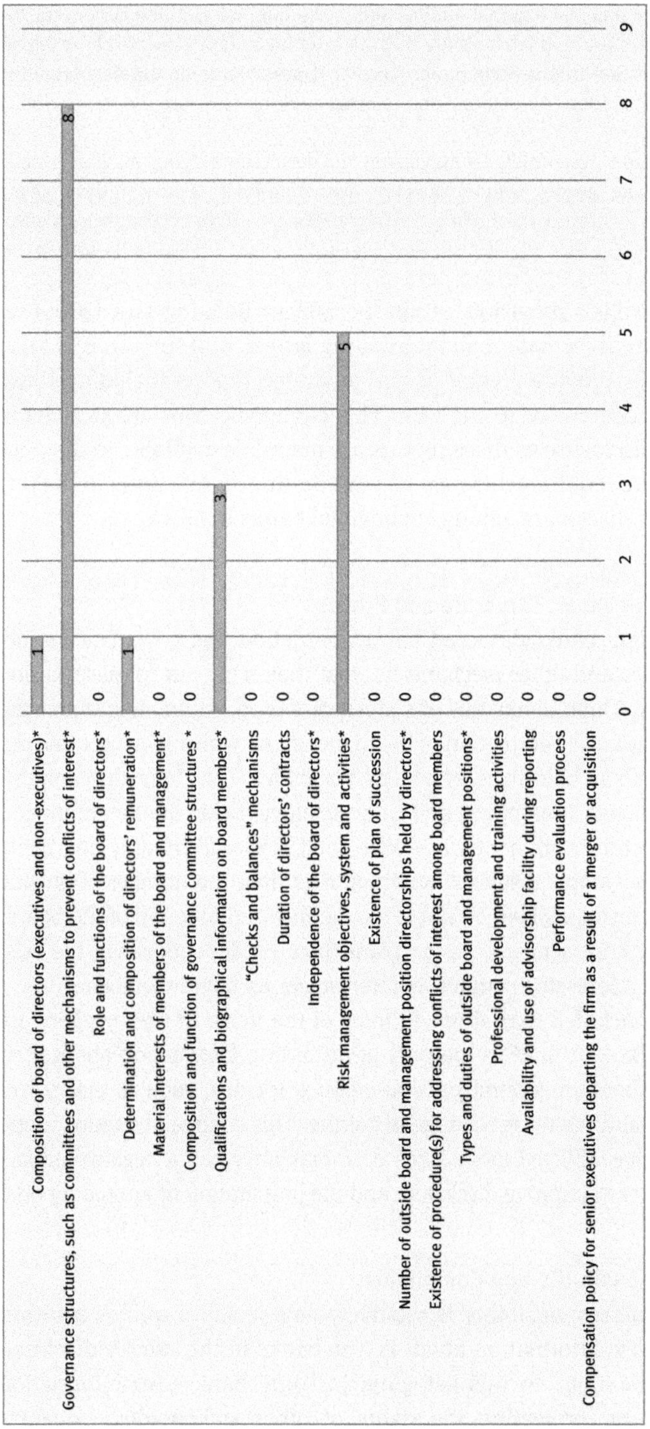

Figure 5.3: Board and Management Structure and Process.

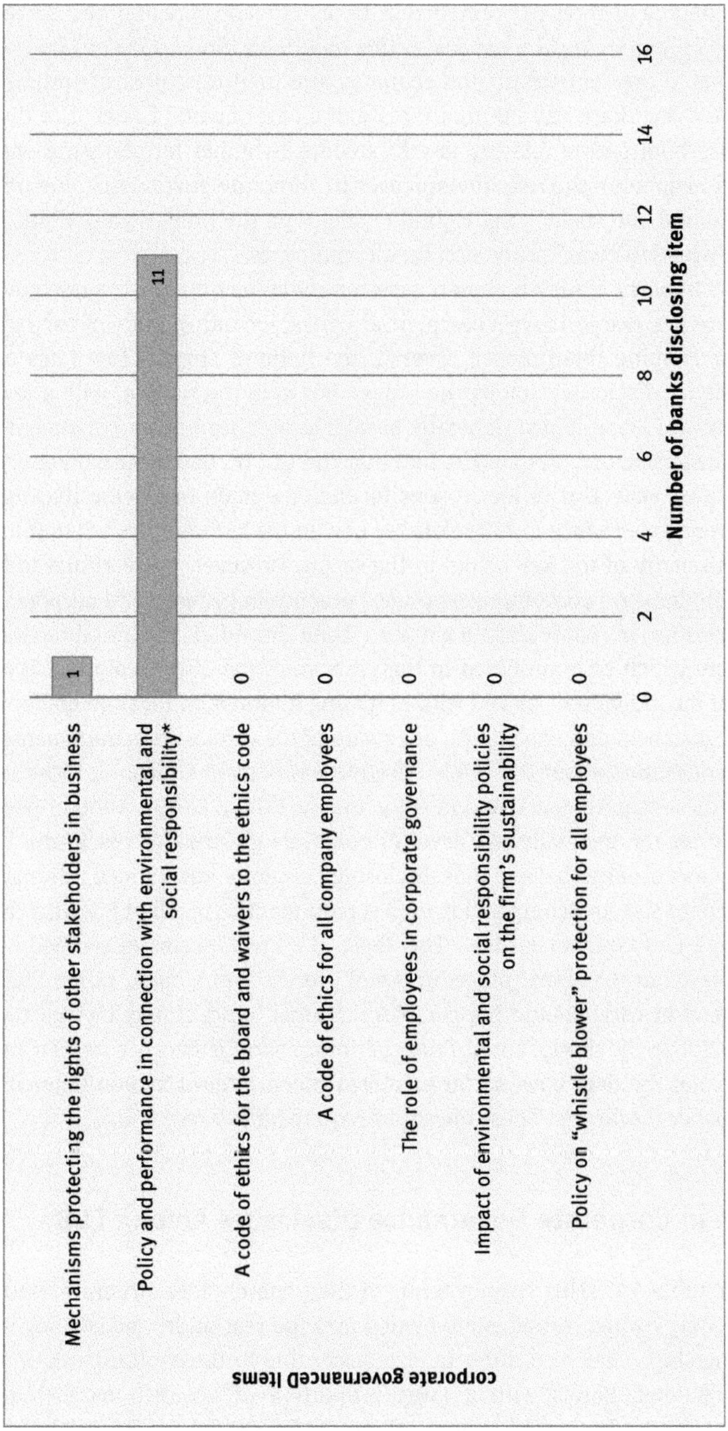

Figure 5.4: Corporate Responsibility and Compliance.

eleven supplied details of their performance in terms of environmental and social responsibility (see Figure 5.4). In most cases, this took the form of a description of their contributions to the community and economy and their treatment of employees, but in no case was there any information about environmental issues. Nor did any bank disclose information relating to ethics codes (whether for company employees or board members), the role of employees in corporate governance, the impact of environmental and social responsibility policies on the firm's sustainability, or its policy on "whistleblower" protection for all employees.

This application of the ISAR benchmark gives an initial picture of corporate governance disclosure practice in Libya's commercial banks, including some of the factors that may be shaping this practice. Overall, the findings suggest low rates of corporate governance disclosure among the sixteen banks in the sample, with a few notable exceptions for some items. Generally speaking, practice among commercial banks remains unsatisfactory, despite the fact that the CGLBS has been mandatory since 2010. There are several possible reasons for this, the main one being that the concept of corporate governance is still relatively new in the LBS and has yet to fully gain traction with many of the key actors in the sector. However, those efforts that have been made to improve corporate governance practice in general, and corporate governance disclosure in particular, have also been impeded by the dramatic changes in culture which have unfolded in the years since the 2011 revolution. It is also possible that the individuals tasked with preparing information for stakeholders, as well as board members and executives, are aware of the disclosure requirements. If so, this raises questions about the CBL's effectiveness both in educating those in the sector about these requirements, and in enforcing the CGLBS (2010). Another possible explanation for the generally low level of corporate governance disclosure is that many key actors seem to believe that disclosing corporate governance information (e.g. about board size and composition etc.) is redundant as much of it is already set out in banking and commercial law. This logic, if correct, seems misguided as users need details about the actual procedures and processes of a bank, rather than a general statement of what should happen. On the other hand, it may be that the reason banks prioritize the disclosure of financial information is because neither inside nor outside stakeholders have so far exhibited much interest in non-financial corporate governance disclosure. These questions require further research.

5.3 Variation in Corporate Governance Disclosure Among LCBs

As illustrated in Table 5.1, LCBs vary in terms of their shareholder structure, with some being privately owned, others state-owned and the rest under mixed Libyan and foreign ownership. They also differ in size, according to the capital bank proportion of acquisitions. Banks with a large proportion of acquisitions include Jumhoriya Bank (43.7%), National Commercial Bank (18.9%), Sahara Bank (14.6%)

and Al-Waha Bank (13.8%), while the rest their proportion of acquisitions are between 1% and 4% out of total capital banking sector (CBL 2012). The banks vary in age, from nine to 55 years old (the oldest being Jumhoriya Bank, National Commercial Bank, Sahara Bank and Al-Waha Bank) and are a mixture of listed and unlisted. Those currently listed in the LSM are Al-Saraya Bank, Jumhoriya Bank, National Commercial Bank, Sahara Bank, Wahada Bank, Commerce and Development Bank and the Mediterranean Bank. Finally, it has been suggested that Libya's commercial banks also differ in terms of their corporate governance practice, ranging from generally weak (the majority) to satisfactory (Zagoub 2011).

Figure 5.5 shows the variation in corporate governance disclosure levels among LCBs, as measured by applying the ISAR benchmark to their most recent annual report and/or website. Interestingly, the figure reveals that the highest level of corporate governance disclosure was achieved by two small and new banks (United Bank and Al-Nuran Bank), one of which disclosed information for ten out of the 52 ISAR disclosure items and the other of which disclosed information for nine. This result appears to contradict Darmadi's (2013) finding that large and old banks disclose more information than small ones, but it is in line with Feldioreanu and Seria's (2015) conclusion that bank size does not appear to influence the value achieved on the corporate governance disclosure index. The lowest level of disclosure was recorded by the Arab Commercial Bank and Al Wafa Bank, each of which provided information for only one item. Three banks disclosed information for five items out of 52, while seven banks disclosed information for six items. The remaining two banks disclosed information for eight and four items. The findings thus indicate a generally low level of corporate governance disclosure among LCBs, with no significant variation.

5.4 Comparison of Corporate Governance Disclosure in LCBs with that in Companies in Other Developing Countries

This section aims to compare the level of corporate governance disclosure in Libya with that found in companies in other developing countries (research question 3). This was done by comparing the data gathered in the present study with data from UNCTAD's 2011 survey of disclosure practices in 22 other developing countries. As UNCTAD's data focus on the practices of the ten largest enterprises in each country, they were compared with the data from the ten best-performing LCBs, as measured against the ISAR benchmark (see Table 5.2). To facilitate the comparison, total average scores were calculated for the LCBs and for the remaining 22 countries. The LCB scores were calculated using the data from the annual reports and websites, while those for the other developing countries were calculated from the data published by the UN (ISAR 2011). The results indicate that in each of the five disclosure categories, Libya scored lowest among the 23 countries, with LCBs disclosing information on an average of 1.9 items in the ownership structure and exercise of control

Figure 5.5: Variation in Corporate Governance Disclosure among Libyan Commercial Banks.

Table 5.2: Total Average Corporate Governance Disclosure by LCBs Compared to Other Developing Countries.

	Ownership structure and exercise of control rights	Financial transparency	Auditing	Corporate responsibility and compliance	Board and management structure and process	Total average
Libya	1.9	3.1	0	1.1	1.8	1.58
Morocco	5.5	4.3	3.8	1.8	7.2	4.52
Egypt	3.0	4.7	3.7	2.7	8.9	4.6
Republic of Korea	5.5	5.2	3.1	5.4	12.2	6.28
Israel	5.4	7.2	4.1	3.3	11.2	6.24
Russian Federation	6.8	7.0	5.2	3.3	11.2	6.7
Chile	6.6	7.1	4.4	3.8	13.3	7.04
Mexico	5.8	7.3	4.6	5.4	12.5	7.12
China	6.7	6.3	4.9	3.0	15.3	7.24
Brazil	6.6	6.3	5.4	5.4	12.8	7.3
Turkey	7.0	6.4	5.8	3.7	13.7	7.32
Poland	7.1	6.9	5.7	3.1	14.1	7.38
Indonesia	5.5	6.6	5.6	5.6	14.4	7.54
South Africa	5.4	6.4	5.6	4.5	15.9	7.56
India	5.6	6.2	6.4	5.5	16.1	7.96
Philippines	6.7	6.8	7.5	3.7	15.6	8.06
Argentina	8.0	6.5	6.3	5.0	16.5	8.46
Malaysia	6.6	7.0	6.9	4.5	17.5	8.5
Colombia	6.6	7.0	6.2	5.3	17.4	8.5
Czech Republic	8.0	7.2	7.0	5.0	16.0	8.64
Hungary	8.5	6.0	7.3	5.5	16.8	8.82
Peru	7.3	6.8	7.8	5.8	17.3	9
Thailand	7.0	7.5	7.7	5.3	17.9	9.08

rights category, 3.1 items in the financial transparency category, 0 items in the auditing category, 1.1 items in the corporate responsibility and compliance category, and 1.8 items in the board and management structure and process category.

Figure 5.6 shows that the majority of companies in UNCTAD's survey disclosed between 35 and 45 items, with only six countries disclosing fewer than 35 items. On average, the companies in UNCTAD's sample disclosed about 35 items or two-thirds of the ISAR benchmark. This contrasts strongly with the picture in the LBS, where none of the commercial banks disclosed more than eleven items. This suggests that on average, Libya has the lowest level of corporate governance disclosure among the developing countries; interestingly, it is behind other countries with similar economic and social cultures, such as Egypt and Morocco.

There are a number of possible reasons for this, including a weak, and in places outdated, legal and regulatory framework, an opaque economic structure, poor accounting, auditing and financial reporting standards, political interference, social and cultural factors and low levels of stakeholder activism. The novelty of corporate governance in Libya means that the country's corporate governance framework is still under-developed compared to those of its neighbours (Larbsh 2010), with the result that accountability and responsibility processes remain weak. However, the tertiary education system is ill-equipped to improve general understanding of corporate governance in Libya because of poor-quality teaching, lack of curricula, lack of infrastructure and structural problems within the sector (Porter and Yergin 2006).

Magrus (2012) also highlights the adverse impact of poor leadership, lack of training among directors and weak awareness among investors. Zagoub (2011) indicates that corporate governance practice and reform in LCBs have primarily been driven by the CBL and Libyan banking legislation, and that these institutional pressures have had more impact in some banks than in others. His study concludes that the CBL needs to put more pressure on LCBs to improve corporate governance, and to offer greater support.

In terms of disclosure specifically, Ellabbar (2007) attributes the poor performance of Libyan companies to cultural influences. He notes the widespread tendency among Libyan companies to delay publishing financial statements, or to publish without auditing, and the lack of channels (such as financial magazines) for making information readily available to users. Kribat (2009) seems to support Ellabbar's conclusion with his finding that Libyan banks failed to comply fully with mandatory disclosure requirements in any of the years covered in his study (2000–2006).

The picture is not entirely negative, however, as recent studies have noted some signs of improvement in disclosure practice among Libyan companies. Hawashe (2014), for example, found that although the extent of voluntary disclosure is still low, it increased gradually during the period of his study, while Osama (2013) identifies a statistically significant increase in the level of disclosure and transparency in the years following the establishment of the LSM. Like Hawashe,

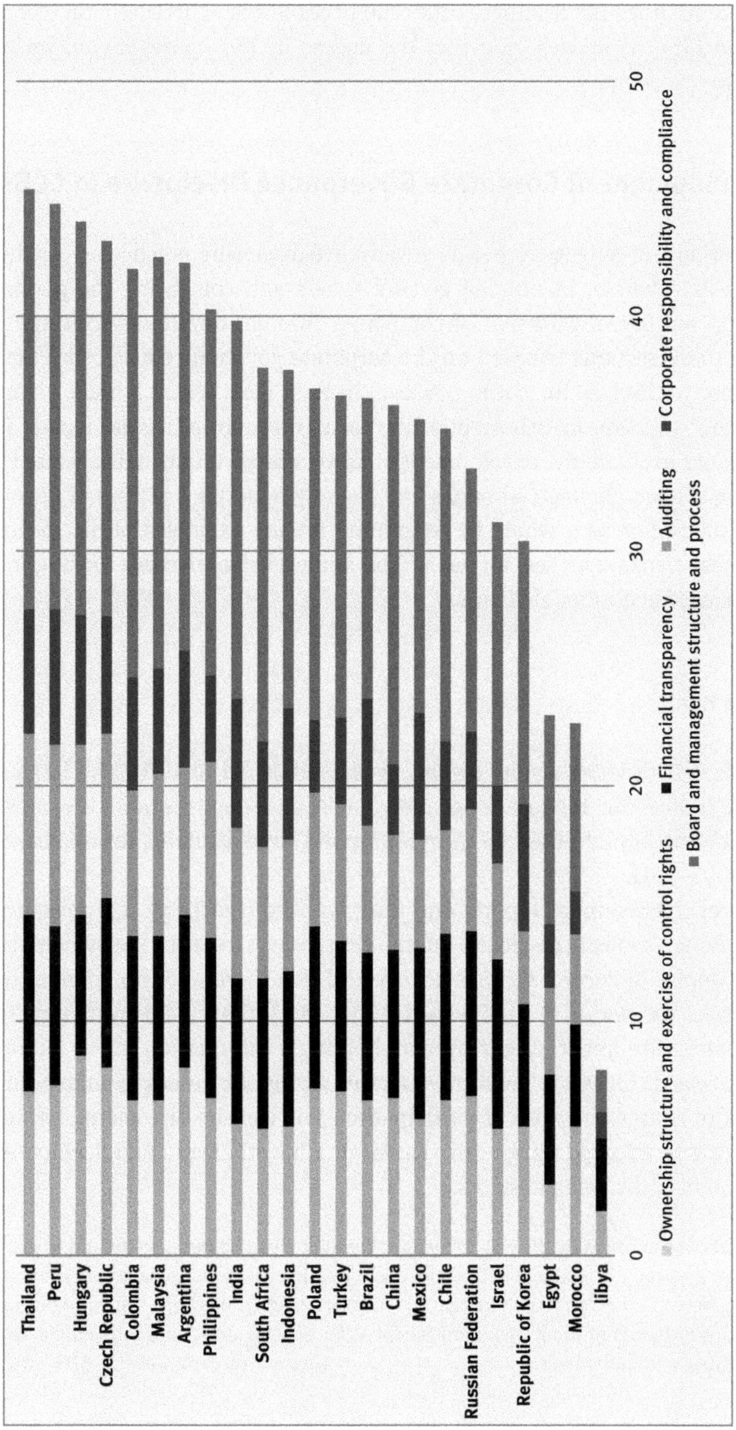

Figure 5.6: Comparison of Libyan commercial Bank Disclosure Practice with that in other Developing Countries.

however, Osama qualifies his findings, cautioning that levels of T&D remain lower in Libya than in other countries, and that the degree of T&D varies significantly from company to company.

5.5 The Development of Corporate Governance Disclosure in LCBs

The previous sections investigate corporate governance disclosure practice across the sample of LCBs as a whole, identifying general trends and comparing the performance of the top ten banks with that of companies in other developing countries. The analysis in these sections is based on the corporate governance disclosure that these banks chose to disclose (or not to disclose) in their most recent annual report or on their current website. In this section, the focus turns to individual banks. It aims to explore and evaluate the development of corporate governance disclosure in eleven of Libya's sixteen commercial banks and thereby build up a picture of development across the sector as a whole by examining textual examples of disclosure published by these banks over several years. The analysis also involves looking for signs of the impact of institutional factors.

5.5.1 Jumhoriya Bank

Jumhoriya Bank, which is 90% state-owned, was established in 1970. The largest bank in Libya, it has the highest assets, revenues and deposits and the most branches (150) of any bank in the LBS. Annual reports were available for this bank for the period 2007–2011.

The review of these annual reports and their website (see Table 5.3) revealed that Jumhoriya Bank's website disclosed information for two items in the ownership structure and exercise of control rights category and that there were no changes to this disclosure over the period of time between 2012–2017; these items were details of shareholder structure and changes in shareholdings. Information about shareholder structure was disclosed in the form of a table giving the names of shareholders, the number of shares and ratio of participation. The website also mentions the policy of privatisation adopted by the CBL. Explaining how the bank had decided to respond to this policy, the website states:

> In line with the plan adopted by the CBL to reconstruct the Libyan banking sector and to reinforce the sector generally to enable it to face any crisis, and in order to keep pace with international developments in the banking industry, Decision No. 26/2008 has been issued to put up one million Libyan dinars of Jumhoriya Bank's capital for general subscription by public and private companies and individuals. (Jumhoriya Bank website, 8/10/2017)

Table 5.3: The Development of Corporate Governance Disclosure in Jumhoriya Bank.

	Annual reports					Website
	2007	2008	2009	2010	2011	(08/10/2017)
Ownership structure and exercise of control rights						2
Financial transparency	2	2	3	3	3	
Auditing	1	1				
Board and management structure and process				2	2	
Corporate responsibility and compliance	1	1	1	1	1	
Total	**4**	**4**	**4**	**6**	**6**	**2**

The disclosure shows the impact of the government's privatisation and political/economic openness programme and suggests that in this bank, the CBL plays the key role in shaping policy.

With the help of the Internet Archive's Wayback Machine it was possible to visit web pages published between 2012 and 2017. There were no changes over this period for two of these items.

Under the category of financial transparency, Jumhoriya Bank, like the other commercial banks in the LBS, disclosed information on its financial and operating results in its annual reports between 2007 and 2011. It was also one of twelve banks to disclose information about its critical accounting estimates, revealing how it calculates its provisions for public and doubtful debts. Table 5.3 indicates that from 2009 onwards, it began to disclose on a third item in this group: the company's objectives. According to the bank's 2011 annual report,

> [t]he bank's management discloses all future development plans. In addition, it provides information to the LSM about any changes in the board and management.
>
> (Jumhoriya Bank Annual Report 2011, p. 10)

This disclosure shows the importance of the LSM as the main information user; the bank was aiming to send a message that it is transparent with the LSM and that full information is available in relation to any change in corporate governance.

The bank's disclosure elsewhere highlights the effect political change has had on its strategic objectives. According to its 2011 annual report,

> [t]he bank's strategy at the beginning of 2011 was to continue with the 2008–2012 strategic plan. However, the 17th February revolution forced the executive management to adopt an emergency plan to protect depositors and owners' money. This became the main goal for that period of time, along with achieving a minimum profit to cover expenses.
>
> (Jumhoriya Bank Annual Report 2011, p. 8)

The revolution and the ensuing political turbulence seem to have created uncertainty for banks, making it much more difficult for them to formulate long-term strategic plans and forcing them to fall back on emergency planning.

In the auditing category, the bank disclosed information only about its internal control systems, and then only in its annual reports for 2007 and 2008. Disclosure on items in the board and management structure and process group began in 2010, continuing into 2011. It disclosed on two items in this group; the first of these was governance structures such as committees and other mechanisms that it has put in place to prevent conflicts of interest. The bank began providing information about board meetings in 2010 with the brief announcement that "[t]he board held eleven meetings in 2010. Discussions covered development and credit activities, and 124 decisions were taken" (Jumhoriya Bank Annual Report 2010, p. 4).

In 2011, the entry was less specific, although this is perhaps understandable given the circumstances. The annual report for that year explained that

"In 2011, the CBL established an interim board to work for six months. This had several meetings which impacted positively on the bank's performance during that period of time" (Jumhoria Bank Annual Report 2011, p. 4).

The fact that the bank began reporting information on corporate governance issues in 2010 may be attributable to the launch of the mandatory corporate governance code in that year. This code obliged banks to reconstruct their boards to meet the corporate governance requirements, but the changes to the board (i.e. its wholesale replacement by the CBL) described in the 2011 annual report were triggered by the bigger political changes that followed the February revolution. This revolution brought with it a new ideology, and many board members and executives who were reluctant to let go of the old socialist attitudes were replaced. In the same year, the bank began to disclose information about its compliance with corporate governance principles: "The bank's management is committed to applying the rules of corporate governance, and to maintaining a high degree of transparency and disclosure towards Libyan society, shareholders, customers and employees." (Jumhoria Bank Annual Report 2011, p. 8)

The bank's promise demonstrates a stakeholder-oriented approach towards corporate governance disclosure that extends beyond shareholders alone.

The second item in this category for which the bank disclosed information was its risk management objectives, system and activities. The 2009 annual report (Jumhorya Bank Annual Report 2009, p. 38) states that

- after merging the two banks, the credit risk sector has been reconstructed to support the bank and confirm the integrity of the credit portfolio.

- the bank capital has been increased to withstand any financial risks. The capital has been increased to a million dinars, supporting the bank's ability to carry out its work and guaranteeing the safety of stakeholders, particularly depositors.
- during 2008, for the first time, marketing's credit and the granting of a credit department have been separated, and new policies have been adopted which take into account the separation between their duties.
- a new executive unit has been established for risk management to confirm the integrity of credit decisions and whether they are in line with the bank's credit policies and Libyan Central Bank regulations.

In the category of corporate responsibility and compliance, Jumhoriya Bank, like most banks in the sample, disclosed information for only one item: policy and performance in connection with environmental and social responsibility. This disclosure took the form of a general statement about the bank's intentions towards its customers, employees and the community at large. Thus, the 2010 annual report claims that

> [t]he bank contributes to the Libyan economy. It has branches and agencies across much of the country and is able to help small and medium enterprises in different areas, including remote areas, by providing them with the financing they need.
>
> (Jumhorya Bank Annual Report 2010, p. 4)

In summary, despite evidence of a slight improvement in disclosure, Jumhoriya Bank's performance in this area remains very weak. Over the last ten years, the bank has demonstrated a tendency to comply only with minimum requirements; it only began reporting on corporate governance when the CGLBS became mandatory in 2010, and its annual reports and web pages have been limited to mandatory items. What corporate governance disclosure it does offer is stakeholder-oriented and relates to bank objectives, changes in shareholdings, ownership structure and the governance structures it has put in place to prevent conflicts of interest. As a state-owned bank which has just recently started to sell its shares in the LSM, the main forces shaping its corporate governance disclosure and practice are the CBL and the LSM. The programme of economic openness adopted by the previous regime appears to have had a positive impact on the bank, but this impact has been undermined to some extent by the dramatic political changes since 2011.

5.5.2 Wahada Bank

The second-largest bank in Libya, the majority state-owned Wahada Bank was established in 1970 with the merger of four banks (the African Arab Bank Company, the Bank of North Africa, Al-Kafela Bank and the Commercial Bank) (Wahada Bank Annual Report 2010). In 2008, the bank joined with the Foreign Bank, acquiring 19% of its shares. The review of the bank's web pages (2012–2017) and annual reports (2007–2010) revealed how its corporate governance disclosure has developed over the last ten years (see Table 5.4).

Wahada Bank has only disclosed information about its ownership structure and exercise of control rights since 2012. This has been limited to one item (ownership structure), with the disclosure appearing on the bank's website:

> Wahada Bank is a Libyan shareholding company, established under Law 153 of 22/12/1970. Paid capital is (432) million LYD. The Social Economic Development Fund owns 54.1% of the stock, the private sector owns 26.9%, the Arab Bank [strategic partner] owns 19%.
>
> (Wahada Bank website 9/10/2017)

In the financial transparency category, Wahada Bank disclosed information in its annual reports only on its financial and operating results and its company objectives. These objectives were first set out in 2008 (Wahada Bank Annual Report 2008, p. 10) and remained unchanged in 2009 and 2010. These objectives were/are:

- To be a pioneer in the provision of outstanding banking services
- To manage the bank's funds effectively
- To expand employees' abilities to work in different banking fields
- To achieve a good score on the bank performance indicator
- To increase the efficiency of banking operations
- To apply the International Accounting Standards in banking management activities
- To increase customer confidence by improving our services
- To enhance employees' skills

The list of objectives shows the competitive tendency of the bank. This competitiveness is a necessary response to the stock market and the government's openness

Table 5.4: The Development of Corporate Governance Disclosure in Wahada Bank.

	Annual reports				Website 9/10/2017
	2007	2008	2009	2010	2017
Ownership structure and exercise of control rights					1
Financial transparency	2	3	3	3	
Auditing					
Board and management structure and process				1	
Corporate responsibility and compliance	1	1	1	1	1
Total	**3**	**4**	**4**	**5**	**2**

programme, which has allowed entry into the LBS of new private and foreign banks. The announcement that the bank was aiming to implement the International Accounting Standards suggests a desire to work towards best practice.

No information was disclosed in either the reports or websites under the auditing category, and there was disclosure for just one item in the board and management structure and process category. This was in the 2010 annual report, when the bank disclosed information about the three main types of risk it faced in that year:

- Credit risks: As a result of the closure of the credit department and branch managers allowing loans and failing to monitor troubled debts, repayments and investment opportunities have been missed.
- Liquidity risks: Owing to the CBL's lack of a liquidity management policy, the bank has faced liquidity risks which have left it unable to meet its obligations in the short term.
- Reputation risks: The bank has faced a reputation risk as a result of inadequate computer systems negatively impacting on the bank's customer service. (Wahada Bank Annual Report 2010, p. 11)

The bank was thus facing difficulties even before the revolution.

Table 5.4 shows that the bank also disclosed information for only one item under the corporate responsibility and compliance category during the period between 2012 and 2017. This was its policy and performance in connection with environmental and social responsibility, which was disclosed in its annual report between 2007 and 2010 and on its website from 2012 onward. Like the previous bank, Wahada Bank offers a general statement about the bank's intentions towards its customers, employees and the wider community. In its website, it proclaims its intention to support the national economy thus: "Wahada Bank's strategic vision is to draw on its history, reputation and efficiency to help the national economy to meet the global economic challenges." (Wahada Bank website 9/10/2017)

Overall, the review revealed no significant improvement in Wahada Bank's corporate governance disclosure in its annual reports over the period 2007–2010. Furthermore, despite its stated ambition to work towards best practice, examination of the bank's web pages over the period 2012–2017 showed that no real progress has been made since the revolution either.

5.5.3 Sahara Bank

With a network of 48 branches covering all the main regions of the country, Sahara Bank is one of Libya's largest public banks (Sahara Bank website 11/10/2017). The bank is a mixed ownership bank; it was created in 1964, but in 2007, it became the first financial institution in Libya to enter into a strategic partnership with a foreign

Table 5.5: The Development of Corporate Governance Disclosure in Sahara Bank.

	Annual reports				Website 09/10/2017
	2007	2008	2009	2010	
Ownership structure and exercise of control rights	2	2	2	2	
Financial transparency	3	3	3	3	1
Auditing					
Board and management structure and process	1				
Corporate responsibility and compliance	1	1	1	1	
Total	**7**	**6**	**6**	**6**	**1**

bank – the BNP Paribas Group. Annual reports for Sahara Bank were available for 2007–2010, while websites were available for 2017 and 2017 (see Table 5.5).

As indicated in Table 5.5, Sahara Bank disclosed information for two items under the ownership structure and exercise of control rights category in its annual reports for 2007–2010. These two items were ownership structure and changes in shareholdings. The bank presented its merger with BNP Paribas as a golden opportunity for expanding its services: "The merger with our new foreign partner (BNP PARIBAS) will add value to our banking service as this bank has many branches (85) around the world." (Sahara Bank Annual Report 2008, p. 4)

And in 2010 the bank declared that

> [a]t the end of the financial year 2010, the General Assembly of the Bank approved the increase of the Bank's capital through the distribution of bonus shares to the shareholders by 50% of the shares. This procedure was implemented at the beginning of the financial year 2011. However, the second phase, an increase of 368 million dinars to the capital of the Bank through the IPO has stopped as result of revolution in the country.
>
> (Sahara Bank Annual Report 2010 p. 1)

Like the previous banks, Sahara Bank discloses its objectives, which seem to be both economic and social. According to its website: "We aim to be one of the national economic pillars and a key player in economic development, and to enhance banking credibility" (Sahara Bank website 9/10/2017). The commitment to economic development was also emphasised back in 2010: "Our Mission is to achieve excellence in our products and business dealings and to be a supporter and partner for development projects and construction." (Sahara Bank Annual Report 2010 p. 4) These examples of disclosure suggest that this bank's strategy for remaining competitive is to focus on the quality of its banking services.

Table 5.5 indicates that between 2007 and 2017, there was just one example of disclosure in the board and management structure and process category. This was in the 2007 annual report and was related to governance structures for preventing conflicts of interest. The report simply states: "The board was reconstructed after the entry of the foreign bank as a strategic partner on 19/9/2007." (Sahara Bank Annual Report 2007, p. 1)

This brief example highlights the importance of the foreign partner as the motivation behind the reconstruction. From the few examples of disclosure that were available, it appears that Sahara Bank is poor at disclosing corporate governance information, but that the foreign partner plays an essential role in the bank's activities, including its corporate governance.

Finally, in terms of corporate responsibility and compliance, Sahara Bank also disclosed information for only one item: policy and performance in connection with environmental and social responsibility. In its annual reports between 2007 and 2010, it gave general information regarding employees and other social contributions. In 2008, this took the form of a discussion of the importance of its staff training programme:

> There is no doubt that several factors contributed to the success of the bank in the light of the development witnessed in terms of infrastructure and training of the bank's existing staff to cope with the world around us [. . .] 540 employees have been trained (an average of two training courses for each employee). (Sahara Bank Annual Report 2008 pp. 5–6)

5.5.4 National Commercial Bank

The National Commercial Bank was established in 1970 as a state-owned bank, but in 2010 it issued 15% of its shares for trading in the LSM. Annual reports were available for the bank for 2007–2010, while web pages were available for 2014–2017. Table 5.6 shows that like the previous banks, the National Commercial Bank disclosed information on only a few items during the research period. These items were: ownership structure, company objectives, governance structures, such as committees and other mechanisms to prevent conflicts of interest, risk management objectives, system and activities, and policy and performance in connection with environmental and social responsibility. In relation to ownership structure, the bank's 2017 website states that:

> [t]he Central Bank of Libya is the key shareholder in the National Commercial Bank. The transactions of the National Commercial Bank are conducted in accordance with the CBL's monetary, credit and financial policies, with the exchange and interest rates it sets out, and in compliance with all applicable laws and regulations.
> (National Commercial Bank website, 15/10/2016)

Table 5.6: The Development of Corporate Governance Disclosure in National Commercial Bank.

	Annual reports				Website
	2007	**2008**	**2009**	**2010**	**15/10/2017**
Ownership structure and exercise of control rights					1
Financial transparency	2	2	2	3	1
Auditing					
Board and management structure and process		1			1
Corporate responsibility and compliance					1
Total	**2**	**3**	**2**	**3**	**4**

The CBL is thus confirmed as the main owner of the bank and the controller of all its policies. Through the CBL, the state shapes corporate governance in this bank. The bank reveals its objective as being

> to realise the highest possible standards in the services and products that we offer so that the National Commercial Bank becomes the benchmark by which the banking sector measures its performance. (National Commercial Bank website 15/10/2017)

The scale of the bank's ambition is expressed in its mission statement in its 2010 annual report:

> The National Commercial Bank aims to make a name for itself on the local, regional and international stages by offering high-value products and services to its clients and shareholders.

We also strive here at the National Commercial Bank to make a difference in everything we do: to be the leads in the local market, and to provide high-quality services based on the needs of customers and the market. (National Commercial Bank Annual Report 2010, p.2)

Like Sahara Bank, the National Commercial Bank sees its offer of high-quality banking services as its best way of remaining competitive. However, the disclosure shows that this bank also wants to play a role in improving the local economy. Demonstrating that its objectives are stakeholder-oriented, in 2010 it declared that

> [w]e seek to get the maximum revenues in the long term, and to protect the best interests of our shareholders and stakeholders through the hard work of our team and a positive work environment. (National Commercial Bank Annual Report 2010, p.2)

The bank began reporting on its governance structures for preventing conflicts of interest on its website in 2014, explaining that

> [t]he governance of the banking sector and that of the National Commercial Bank in particular require the adoption of transparency. The senior and executive management of the bank, along with all the administrative levels, place a high priority on the practice and implementation of sound corporate governance in the sector at both domestic and international levels. The National Commercial Bank is committed to applying the best practices described in the recommendations of the Basel Committee on Corporate Governance, and to complying with the requirements and instructions of the banking and financial supervisory authorities. (National Commercial Bank website, 15/10/2017)

This disclosure shows that the bank aims not only to adhere to the legal requirements but also to international best practice. The intention to apply best practice actually goes back further than this; it can be traced back to 2008, when it appeared in the bank's disclosure regarding its risk management objectives, system and activities. The annual report for that year reveals that the bank's aim is to "achieve a comprehensive [risk management] system that is able to compete effectively and meet the risk-related banking standards and laws" (National Commercial Bank Annual Report 2008, p. 38).

Table 5.1 indicates that eleven of the banks in the sample disclosed information on their policy and performance in connection with environmental and social responsibility in their most recent annual report or website. However, in most cases, this was subsumed within more general statements about the bank's intentions towards its customers, employees or the community at large. The National Commercial Bank was the only bank to talk explicitly about the concept of social responsibility and the role this plays in guiding the bank's policy and activities. On its web page dedicated to the topic, the bank asserts:

> Our sense of social responsibility underpins our involvement in the development of local communities. To this end, we give support to educational projects and the development of the education sector by funding schools and contributing to the establishment of computer laboratories across our beloved Libya to help students everywhere in our country be productive and participate in building our national economy.
>
> This modern concept of corporate social responsibility, through which firms and institutions in the private sector help in building and developing local communities, participating in their progress and making a difference, realising achievements and accomplishments in their home country, drives us here at the National Commercial Bank to work tirelessly towards the development of Libya's economy and society. Our work mainly focuses on the education sector, and on funding the educational programmes and processes to strengthen the economy of Libya and raise living standards for our citizens.
>
> At the heart of this is the National Commercial Bank's involvement in the Dates International Exhibition, which aims to highlight the quality of Libyan date products and to open the doors wide for Libyan farmers and exporters so that their products reach international markets.

> The National Commercial Bank was also recently honoured at a banking event held under the slogan "Small and medium enterprises: the strategic option to develop the economy and create job opportunities". The honour recognised the bank's role in fostering national and local entrepreneurial development through its support of SMEs. The forum was organised by the Union of Arab Banks with the cooperation of the Central Bank of Libya and the Arab Union for Small Enterprises. (National Commercial Bank website 15/10/2017)

The review of earlier web pages revealed that this example of disclosure has been reprinted without significant change since 2014.

Overall, the National Commercial Bank discloses information on only a few of the ISAR benchmark items, though there has been a slight improvement since it started reporting about corporate governance on its website in 2014. It appears that the bank is trying to be more transparent with its shareholders, providing a dedicated link for them on its website, and it has also stated its intentions to work towards applying corporate governance best practice and to protect all of its stakeholders.

5.5.5 United Bank

This bank is a joint-stock company, established in 2007 with the merger of three private banks. In 2010, a foreign bank acquired 40% of the bank's shareholding, leaving the remaining 60% with Libyan shareholders. As shown in Table 5.7, annual reports were available for this bank for the years 2007–2013, and web pages were available for 2013–2017. The review of these sources revealed a significant expansion in corporate governance disclosure between 2011 and 2013, but nothing since then.

Within the ownership structure and exercise of control rights group of items, United Bank disclosed information on ownership structure and changes in shareholdings in its reports for 2012 and 2013. The bank's 2013 annual report, for example, explains that

> [t]he United Bank of Commerce and Investment (UBCI) was established following the merger of three national banks. The bank's operation was limited in certain urban areas of the country until the year 2009 when major investors and insurance companies acquired stakes in the bank. (United Bank Annual Report 2013, p. 7)

The report goes on to explain the reasons behind the foreign merger:

> The shareholders saw the need to improve the infrastructure of the bank in order to compete in Libya's booming industrial sector and agreed to look for foreign banks willing to enter into a strategic partnership agreement that would guarantee improvement in the bank's infrastructure and resources over the upcoming years. Three years after its establishment, the bank's stakeholders signed a strategic partnership agreement with Ahli United Bank. One of the leading banking groups in the Kingdom of Bahrain, it has a strong presence in the Middle East and North Africa regions. (United Bank Annual Report 2013, p. 7)

Table 5.7: The Development of Corporate Governance Disclosure in United Bank.

	Annual reports							Websites
	2007	**2008**	**2009**	**2010**	**2011**	**2012**	**2013**	**20/10/2017**
Ownership structure and exercise of control rights						2	2	
Financial transparency	2	2	2	2	2	3	3	
Auditing								
Board and management structure and process						3	3	
Corporate responsibility and compliance	1	1	1	1	1	1	1	
Total	**3**	**3**	**3**	**3**	**3**	**9**	**9**	**0**

The disclosure about the change in shareholdings highlights the importance of the foreign partner in improving the bank's ability to be competitive.

As was the case for the banks discussed above, United Bank disclosed information regarding financial and operating results and critical accounting estimates in its annual reports, adding company objectives in 2012. According to the 2013 annual report, these are

> upgrading services and products to meet customers' expectations; ensuring an appropriate environment for developing the professional capacities of employees; achieving excellent returns for shareholders; and ensuring the bank remains worthy of the title "Best Private Bank in Libya". (United Bank Annual Report 2013, p. 7)

It began reporting within the board and management structure and process group of items in 2012, disclosing information regarding the governance structures it has put in place to prevent conflicts of interest. The bank was at pains to point out that it

> pays great attention to optimising corporate governance practices. The bank's board of directors is responsible for supervising the implementation of all policies and regulations to ensure the best returns are achieved for all stakeholders, including shareholders, customers, employees and more generally, society as a whole. These policies and procedures include the laws and regulations issued by the Central Bank of Libya and the Basel Committee's directives. The bank periodically reviews its governance policies and improves them when necessary.
> (United Bank Annual Report 2013, p. 16)

The extract suggests that the bank sees the application of corporate governance as being in the interests of all stakeholders. Furthermore, in its determination to abide by the directives of both the CBL and the BCBS, it appears to demonstrate a commitment to achieving international best practice. This commitment is expressed clearly in the board's willingness to establish board committees to assist it in its duties:

> The board of directors has formed several committees for special purposes to assist in supervising the bank and to enhance the applied governance procedures. These committees are assigned specific responsibilities and they report periodically to the board of directors. Following each AGM meeting, the board of directors forms its board committees and appoints members. These committees are considered the link between the bank's management and the board of directors. (United Bank Annual Report 2013, p. 16)

The commitment to achieving best practice is also evident in the bank's provision of comprehensive biographical information on all board members and executive managers. This information is a feature of its annual reports in 2012 and 2013. An example is the lengthy statement describing the background and qualifications of the board chairman, Mr Abdulla A. Saudi, published in the annual report of 2013:

> Abdulla Saudi is a world-renowned and respected international banker with over 50 years of experience. He holds a Diploma in Commerce, Management and Accounting. He worked at the Central Bank of Libya for 14 years, holding various positions including that of Manager of the Banking Department and Head of the Foreign Investment Department. He was the founder of the Libyan Arab Foreign Bank, where he served as Executive Chairman between 1972 and 1980, establishing branches of the bank worldwide. He was the founder of the Arab Banking Corporation (B.S.C.), Bahrain and served as its President and Chief Executive from 1980 to 1994. He also founded Arab Financial Services (E.C.), Bahrain in 1982 and ABC Islamic Bank (E.C.) in the early 1980s. Mr Saudi was honoured at Georgetown University in Washington D.C., as a result of being voted one of the "Most Innovative Bankers" by the representatives of governments and international commercial bankers attending the International Monetary Fund and World Bank meetings in 1980. In 1991, he was awarded the accolade "Best Banker" by the Association of Arab-American Banks in New York. He was the first to receive the "Arab Banker of the Year" award, in 1993, from the Union of Arab Banks. In recognition of his role in the development of banking relationships between Arab and European states, Mr. Saudi has been honoured, over his career, with several gold medals and awards, notable amongst which are those bestowed in 1977 by the King of Spain and the President of Italy and the Grand Medal of the Republic of Tunisia in 1993. In 2012, he was awarded the Integrity Award by the Arab Union for Combating Forgery – Subordinate of the Arab League. He is currently the Executive Chairman of ASA Consultants (W.L.L.), Bahrain, Deputy Chairman of Al-Baraka Banking Group/Bahrain, and board member of Credit Libanais/Beirut.
> (United Bank Annual Report 2013, p. 9)

Also in the board management structure and process category, the bank's 2013 annual report devotes a whole page to risk management:

> During 2013, UBCI worked on activating the risk department's role in line with the bank's strategy, CBL regulations, and Basel II requirements. A complete credit policy, along with an executive risk committee, and its roles and responsibilities, were prepared by the risk department and approved by the board of directors. In addition to its work mitigating operational risk, the committee is responsible for restructuring the bank's branches and approving Murabaha financing of more than 15 million Libyan dinars. (United Bank Annual Report 2013, p. 9)

This disclosure offers further evidence that the bank is aiming to meet international standards.

In the corporate responsibility and compliance category, the bank disclosed information on its policy and performance in connection with environmental and social responsibility in each of its annual reports from 2007 to 2013. In its 2013 annual report, for example, it thanks its employees, CBL regulators, customers and investors:

> I would like to seize this opportunity to express my sincere thanks to the Bank's shareholders, regulatory authorities led by the Central Bank of Libya, all our customers including businesses and businessmen and others for their support and understanding. I would also like to express my thanks to all the Bank's employees for enduring a great deal of inconvenience due to the extraordinary conditions. (United Bank Annual Report 2013, p. 12)

United Bank's corporate governance disclosure began in its 2012 annual report with the announcement that it would start implementing reforms in 2013. This report set out the twin aims of United's corporate governance policy as being to provide a high-quality banking service for Libyan customers and to protect shareholders and depositors in line with international standards and Libyan law. Accordingly, it explained that the size of the board would be increased from seven to ten members to meet new legal requirements (United Bank Annual Report 2012, p. 8). The report was also the first to give details of the qualifications and experience of board members and executives. This trend continued in the 2013 annual report, which gives more comprehensive information about the bank's corporate governance practice, such as its creation of board committees. It is an indication of the bank's commitment to work towards best international practice that one of these committees is not compulsory under the CGLBS (2010); in other words, the bank has shown that it is willing to go beyond minimum compliance in terms of its corporate governance disclosure and practice.

5.5.6 Commerce & Development Bank

This is the largest private bank in Libya, with 30 branches across the country. It was established in 1996 without any support from the government. Annual reports for this bank were available only for 2007–2011, but web pages were available for the years 2010–2017.

Table 5.8: The Development of Corporate Governance Disclosure in Commerce & Development Bank.

	Annual reports					Website
	2007	**2008**	**2009**	**2010**	**2011**	**25/10/2016**
Ownership structure and exercise of control rights	1	1	1	1	1	1
Financial transparency	2	2	3	3	3	
Auditing						
Board and management structure and process			1	1	1	
Corporate responsibility and compliance	1	1	1	1	1	
Total	**4**	**4**	**6**	**6**	**6**	**1**

The review of these reports and pages indicated that over this period, the bank gave no information about shareholder structure other than to state the number of natural and juridical persons holding shares (see Table 5.8). As was the case for the other banks, it disclosed its financial and operating results and critical accounting estimates, which appeared in its annual reports up until 2011. It also listed its objectives between 2009 and 2011. According to the annual report for 2011 (Commerce and Development Bank Annual Report 2011, p. 10), these are:

- To satisfy our customers' expectations
- To increase profits and reduce costs to increase stockholders' equity and strengthen the bank's financial position
- To build a sound banking institution, focusing on asset quality
- To recruit, train, motivate and reward talented banking personnel by providing local and foreign training programmes and incentives for the best among them
- To install the single-family spirit in all branches and agencies under the leadership of the bank's top management

Similar statements appear in the annual reports for 2009 and 2010. Once again, by focusing on customers, stockholders and staff in its disclosed objectives, the bank aims to cement its reputation as a stakeholder-oriented organisation.

The only item to feature from the board and management structure and process category is governance structures such as committees and other mechanisms to prevent conflicts of interest. The bank began reporting on its governance structures in its 2009 annual report, declaring that

> [w]here the Board of Directors' activity is governed by Libyan Banking Law No.1/2005, the Bank of Commerce and Development adopts the Institutional Governance Manual, aiming to achieve the principles of institutional governance by the separation of the Board of Directors and executive management in terms of responsibilities and delegation of authority.
>
> (Commerce and Development Bank Annual Report 2009, p. 15)

The same statement is repeated in the annual reports of 2010 and 2011. The example suggests that the main force shaping the Commerce and Development Bank's corporate governance disclosure and practice is the coercive pressure exerted by the law. The bank seems inclined to comply only with the minimum legal requirements, making no mention of best practice or international standards.

Also under the governance structures item, the bank disclosed information about its board meetings in its 2011 annual report, which accounts for the reduced number of board meetings that were held that year:

> The Board of Directors held only three meetings during the year 2011 due to the circumstances that accompanied the revolution and the consequent interruption in communication between East and West Libya and the difficulty of communicating with board members in Tripoli.
>
> (Commerce Development Bank Annual Report 2011, p. 12)

The disclosure reflects the impact the unstable political situation has had on corporate governance in Libya.

In terms of corporate responsibility and compliance, the bank disclosed in its 2011 annual report how it had discharged its environmental and social responsibility during the revolution:

> In spite of the liquidity crisis suffered by most Libyan banks, resulting in some banks having to close their doors to customers, thanks be to God, we were able to provide the withdrawal ceiling amount specified by the Central Bank of Libya, at LYD 750, for all customers of the Bank. Additionally, your Bank provided the vaults of branches of the other banks with a flow of cash to cover their currency needs. Your Bank was the only bank, enabled by its own capability, to operate its Western Union transfers, which played a huge role in solving the problems of citizens, especially those problems of expenses related to medical treatment and study costs abroad, as well as foreign workers in Libya who preferred to remain in the country.
>
> (Commerce and Development Bank Annual Report 2011, p. 11)

To sum up, the Commerce and Development Bank did not start reporting on corporate governance until 2009. Although this is encouraging in that it predates the CGLBS becoming mandatory in 2010, the evidence suggests that corporate governance practice in this bank is largely shaped by the law and the coercive pressure from the CBL. Disclosure is offered on very few of the ISAR benchmark items, and there is no suggestion that the bank is willing to go beyond the minimum level of compliance.

5.5.7 First Gulf Libyan Bank

This is a fully-fledged commercial bank. It is equally owned by the Libyan government and its foreign bank partner. Table 5.9 shows that annual reports were available for this bank for the period 2008–2013 and web pages were available for 2009, 2010, 2013 and 2017; however, review of these sources showed that the bank discloses information on only a few items, and that there has been no significant improvement in terms of corporate governance disclosure and practice over this period.

On the bank objectives item, First Gulf Libyan Bank declares that its aim is

> to be a world class organisation. Striving towards this aim is the philosophy of providing and optimising shareholder, customer and employee value. People focused, in line with its belief that people drive excellence and make the difference, First Gulf Libyan Bank creates opportunities to challenge its workforce and empower it to grow and become world-class.
>
> At First Gulf Libyan Bank, trust and integrity are inherent ethics. Whether it is interaction with colleagues, customers, partners or stakeholders, the Bank builds mutually beneficial and enduring relationships by adhering to these corporate principles.
>
> (First Gulf Libyan Bank website 9/11/2017)

The objectives indicate a stakeholder-oriented bank that is keen to establish a reputation for trustworthiness among its stakeholders. To this end, the website furnishes these stakeholders with reassuring details about the bank's risk management framework:

Table 5.9: The Development of Corporate Governance Disclosure in First Gulf Libyan Bank.

	Annual reports						Website
	2008	2009	2010	2011	2012	2013	9/11/2017
Ownership structure and exercise of control rights							1
Financial transparency	2	2	2	2	2	2	1
Auditing							
Board and management structure and process							1
Corporate responsibility and compliance	1	1	1	1	1	1	1
Total	**3**	**3**	**3**	**3**	**3**	**3**	**4**

> The Bank's risk management policies are established to identify and analyse the risks faced by the Bank, to set appropriate risk limits and controls, and to monitor risks and adherence to limits. The Bank, through its training and management standards and procedures, aims to develop a disciplined and constructive control environment in which all employees understand their roles and obligations. The Bank Audit Committee oversees how management monitors compliance with the Bank's risk management policies and procedures and reviews the adequacy of the risk management framework in relation to the risks faced by the Bank. The Bank Audit Committee is assisted in its oversight role by the Internal Audit.
>
> (First Gulf Libyan Bank website 9/11/2017)

However, while the general level of disclosure of non-financial information is low, the bank does follow international best practice when it comes to its financial reporting; in this instance, it goes beyond minimum compliance. For example, according to the 2011 annual report,

> [t]he financial statements of First Gulf Libyan Bank have been prepared in accordance with the International Financial Reporting Standards (IFRS) as issued by the International Accounting Standards Board (IASB), the interpretations issued by the Standing Interpretation Committee of the IASB, and the domestic regulations and guidelines of the Central Bank of Libya.
>
> (First Gulf Libyan Bank Annual Report 2011, p. 12)

On the issue of corporate responsibility and compliance, First Gulf Libyan Bank, like others in the sample, offers a general statement about social responsibility. These have been published in both the annual reports and on its website. Most recently, its 2017 website states that

> FGLB strives to set standards of excellence, explore new opportunities and pursue innovation. The bank focuses on delivering products and services that address the needs of a dynamic economy, perpetuate progress and meet customer requirements.
>
> (First Gulf Libyan Bank website 9/11/2017)

5.5.8 Al-Saraya Bank

This bank was established in 1997 as the Al-Ahli Bank of Tripoli. In 2007, the bank became a joint-stock company, a new management was installed and it was renamed Al-Saraya Bank. By mid-2016, the bank had five branches. As Table 5.10 indicates, annual reports were available for the period 2007–2013 and web pages were available for 2013–2017. Review of these sources once again indicated that the bank discloses information on very few of the ISAR benchmark items; apart from its financial and operating results, Al-Saraya Bank disclose under three items of this category, financial and operating results, critical accounting estimates and company's objectives. Under the category of Board and Management Structure and Process the bank only discloses information on its governance structures for preventing conflicts of interest and the qualifications of its board members, and regarding to Corporate

Table 5.10: The Development of Corporate Governance Disclosure in Al-Saraya Bank.

	Annual reports							Website 15/11/2017
	2007	**2008**	**2009**	**2010**	**2011**	**2012**	**2013**	**2017**
Ownership structure and exercise of control rights								
Financial transparency	3	3	3	3	3	3	3	
Auditing								
Board and management structure and process								2
Corporate responsibility and compliance								1
Total	**3**	**3**	**3**	**3**	**3**	**3**	**3**	**3**

Responsibility and Compliance, the bank disclose information on its policy and performance in connection with environmental and social responsibility.

In terms of its governance structures, the bank states only that

> [t]he Board of Directors' primary responsibility is to supervise the management of the bank's affairs by providing effective corporate governance. In doing so, the Board aims to balance the interests of the bank's diverse constituencies, including its shareholders, customers, employees and responsibility to the communities in which we operate.
>
> (Al-Saraya Bank website 15/11/2017)

As with the other banks in the sample, the disclosure is designed to display a stakeholder-oriented approach towards corporate governance, making explicit Al-Saraya Bank's commitment to balance the various interests of its shareholders, customers, employees and the wider community. The bank is one of the few to provide sufficient information about the qualifications and background of its board members on its website. The 2011 annual report reveals that the board met eight times that year and that "[d]ecisions were taken in relation to the appointment of the chairman of the board and senior managers" (Al-Saraya Bank Annual Report 2011, p. 3).

The single item disclosed in the corporate responsibility and compliance category is the bank's policy and performance in connection with environmental and social responsibility. This disclosure takes the form of a brief statement describing the bank's wish to foster the professional development of its employees: "We treat our employees with trust and respect. Because we believe in what we do, we are always ready to give them the best and make the greatest effort to help them enhance their skills." (Al-Saraya Bank website 15/11/ 2017)

The same statement appears in each version of the bank's website between 2013 and 2017. Overall, the review of Al-Saraya Bank's reports and websites demonstrated no improvement in its disclosure practice over the research period.

5.5.9 North Africa Bank

North Africa Bank is predominantly state-owned, with just 18% of the bank in private hands (see Table 3.2). The bank, which holds capital of 350 million Libyan dinars, already provides its services through 54 branches and agencies scattered all over the country and has plans to expand its network even further. However, the review of its annual reports (for the period 2007–2008) and web pages (for the period 2013–2017) revealed that there was no significant improvement in its corporate governance disclosure over the research period; since 2013, North Africa Bank has disclosed information on only one item, in the financial transparency category (see Table 5.11).

Information about one item in the ownership structure and exercise of control rights category was disclosed in the bank's 2008 annual report, when it acknowledged the change in shareholding occasioned by its merger with other institutions:

> The bank is complying with Decision No. 1/2006 in its merger with 21 private banks. Two banks completed the merger procedures during 2007 and by the end of 2008, eleven banks will have been merged with our bank. (North Africa Bank Annual Report 2008 p. 2)

The bank disclosed information on three items in the financial transparency category in its annual reports for 2007 and 2008. These included financial and

Table 5.11: The Development of Corporate Governance Disclosure in North Africa Bank.

	Annual reports		Website 20/11/207
	2007	2008	2017
Ownership structure and exercise of control rights		1	
Financial transparency	3	3	1
Auditing			
Board and management structure and process			
Corporate responsibility and compliance	1	1	
Total	**4**	**5**	**1**

operating results, critical accounting estimates and its objectives. More recently, the bank's disclosure in terms of its objectives has been geared towards its decision to start offering its customers Islamic financial services. Hence, on its 2017 website, it announced:

> The bank intends to provide banking services in conformity with the Islamic legal code in two branches [. . .] We are looking forward to being pioneers in the world of financial services and to providing our customers with the widest ranging and highest quality services in accordance with the Islamic legal code, delivered with professionalism by highly skilled banking experts. We intend to employ advanced technology in our management, operating and customer service functions to develop a highly skilled staff that is able to respond to our customers' requirements in the most effective way possible. (North Africa Bank website 20/11/2017)

Table 5.11 shows that the bank disclosed information for just one item in the corporate responsibility and compliance category during the research period. This disclosure, regarding its policy and performance in connection with environmental and social responsibility, appeared in the 2007 and 2008 reports. However, the information now being provided by the bank about its Islamic banking services is arguably being presented as evidence of its commitment to social responsibility, for example in its promise to employ staff

> who promise to devote their efforts and time to give the best service they can to the bank's customers according to the Regulations of the Legal Authority on Islamic Services, according to the Islamic code. (North Africa Bank website 20/11/2017)

Like the previous banks, North Africa Bank aims to distinguish itself by emphasising the quality of the service it offers, but unlike the previous banks, it is also seeking to enhance its legitimacy and reputation by adopting Sharia-based rules.

5.5.10 Al-Amman Bank

Al-Amman Bank started out as a private company, originally owned entirely by Libyan shareholders. It was one of the first banks to be established after the CBL gave permission for private commercial banks to start operating in the LBS (with the issue of Banking Law No. 1/1993, later replaced by Banking Law No.1/2005). The bank is now owned 60% by private Libyan shareholders, with the remaining 40% being held by foreign partners. The review of the bank's annual reports (covering the period 2007–2008) (see Table 5.12) revealed a very low level of corporate governance disclosure (on financial and operating results only), but there was slightly more disclosure on its website (available for the period 2013–2017).

Describing its ownership structure, one version of the bank's 2016 website explains:

Table 5.12: The Development of Corporate Governance Disclosure in Al-Amman Bank.

	Annual reports		Website
	2007	2008	22/11/2017
Ownership structure and exercise of control rights			2
Financial transparency	1	1	
Auditing			
Board and management structure and process			1
Corporate responsibility and compliance			1
Total			**3**

> Since the development of the Al-Amman Bank is a consistent goal of its founders whether in terms of financial position or expanding its services and competition capabilities, in 2010, Al-Amman Bank entered into a strategic partnership with Banco Espirito Santo from Portugal, one of the largest banks in Europe, increasing Al-Amman Bank's capital to 100,020,000 LYD.

Al-Amman Bank is now 40% Portuguese-owned by Banco Espirito Santo, and 60% Libyan-owned by the Libyan private sector. The Portuguese partner is in charge of the executive management and represented by four members of the Board of Directors alongside three Libyan Board members including the Chairman. Al-Amman Bank is now part of the international BES Group. (Al-Amman Bank website 22/11/2017)

The website was subsequently amended to record the change in shareholding when this partnership ended:

> Al-Amman Bank has ended its partnership with Banco Espirito Santo. The 40% shares of the previous partner have been acquired by Freslake Limited with the same fully paid share capital in the order of 100,020,000 LYD. (Al-Amman Bank website 22/11/2017)

None of the websites contain anything in the financial transparency or auditing categories, but in the board and management structure and process category, they give information about the governance structures the bank has in place to prevent conflicts of interest. Thus, the 2016 version of the site asserts that

> Al-Amman Bank's corporate governance model fully complies with the Libyan legal framework and the Central Bank of Libya's (CBL) regulations and Corporate Governance Framework for the Banking System. (Al-Amman Bank website 22/11/2017)

Once again, the disclosure suggests that corporate governance in the bank has been influenced primarily by legal obligations. There is no indication on the website that Al-Amman Bank has any interest in going beyond the minimum corporate

governance requirements. Describing the structure of its governance, the bank explains that it is based on three pillars (Al-Amman Bank website 22/11/ 2017):
- A Board of Directors that is in charge of the overall strategy and of monitoring its execution by management
- A General Manager and his team, responsible for leading the executive management of the bank and executing the strategic plan
- A Control Committee that monitors the work and results of the Board of Directors and the General Manager and his team

Finally, the website adds that "[t]he Board of Directors is composed of nine members, including a Chairman and Deputy Chairman and seven Members" (Al-Amman Bank website 22/11/2017).

5.5.11 Al-Nuran Bank

This is a new bank, first established in 2008 but only operating since 2015. Al-Nuran Bank is a joint-stock Libyan company with a capital of 600 million dinars divided equally between the Libyan Foreign Bank and the Qatari Bank (Al-Nuran Bank website, 25/11/2017). The sole information source for this bank was its website, published in 2016 and 2017. Although the bank disclosed on only ten out of the 52 items in the ISAR benchmark on these sites, it achieved a higher level of corporate governance disclosure, especially in regard to board and management structure and process, than the other banks in the sample. The site published information for items in four of the five ISAR categories: ownership structure and exercise of control rights, financial transparency, board and management structure and process and corporate responsibility and compliance.

As Table 5.13 reveals, in the first of these categories, the bank disclosed information on two items. On the issue of ownership structure, the 2017 website states that

Table 5.13: The Development of Corporate Governance Disclosure in Al-Nuran Bank.

	Websites 25/11/2017
Ownership structure and exercise of control rights	2
Financial transparency	2
Auditing	
Board and management structure and process	5
Corporate responsibility and compliance	1
Total	**10**

> [t]he Bank's subscribed capital is 600 million Libyan dinars, divided into 60 million shares, the value per share ten Libyan dinars paid upon incorporation: from the Libyan Foreign Bank 30 million shares totalling 300 million L.D, and Qatar holding 30 million shares totalling 300 million L.D. (Al-Nuran Bank website, 25/11/2017)

On the other item, Al-Nuran Bank was the only bank in the sample to disclose information about the process for holding annual general meetings:

> The Ordinary General Assembly of Parties and Extraordinary AP held their meetings last August 14, 2015. An announcement was made regarding the appointment of the Board of Directors. Consideration was also given to the Board of the Bank's report of its activity for the years 2013 and 2014; the financial statements and Auditors' report and the ratification thereof; the discharge of the Board of Directors; and the Sharia Supervisory Board's report for the years 2013 and 2014. In addition, External Auditors were chosen to review the financial statements of the Bank for the years 2015 and 2016, in accordance with the statute, and their fees were determined. (Al-Nuran Bank website 25/11/2016)

Table 5.13 shows that in the financial transparency group, the bank disclosed information on two items in 2016 and 2017. Al-Nuran Bank, like almost all of the other banks, disclosed information about its objectives and, also like most of the other banks, this disclosure was designed to show that it is stakeholder-oriented:

> We aim to build partnerships with all our stakeholders including employees, customers, businesses, suppliers, shareholders – these relationships are the foundation of our business. We will never compromise on our principles or our transparency as these are what make these relationships durable. (Al-Nuran Bank website 25/11/2017)

However, the bank was ahead of the others in its willingness to disclose information about the board's responsibilities regarding financial communications. According to the 2017 website,

> [t]he Bank follows a clear policy towards communicating information on its activities and business to all its shareholders and related parties. It endorses a communication disclosure policy consistent with the requirements of the Basel Convention 2; the Assembly of Parties of the Bank holds an annual meeting, attended by the Chairman and members of the Board of Directors, representatives of the official authorities and Auditors, to review the financial results and respond to questions and inquiries from shareholder.
> (Al-Nuran Bank website 25/11/2017)

The bank disclosed information for five items in the board and management structure and process group in both 2016 and 2017. This was also the only bank to disclose information about the composition of the board of directors, though it made no mention of the balance of executives and non-executives. The 2016 website explains:

> The Bank's Board of Directors consists of ten members appointed in accordance with the provisions of the Statute of the Bank in line with the amended banking law. The Bank's Board consists of members with the relevant professional background and work experience. Members are selected based on their professional experience in accordance with the Institutional Control Charter requirements (Corporate Governance Guide). Appointment to the Board is subject to the approval of the Central Bank of Libya.
>
> (Al-Nuran Bank website 25/11/2017)

As this example highlights, the bank provided information about the qualifications and background of board members, emphasising particularly their experience. This professional experience may be one reason why Al-Nuran Bank is already able to achieve higher quality corporate governance disclosure and practice than its competitors.

Describing the governance structures the bank has in place to prevent conflicts of interest, the 2017 website insists that

> [p]rotecting the rights of shareholders and adding value to their ownership in the Bank will always be a priority of Al-Nuran Bank, which it will achieve through the application of professional banking practices. The Bank will not only apply the State and regulators' laws (including the Corporate Governance Guide issued by the Central Bank of Libya and the Bank's own Institutional Control Charter), it will also seek to learn from the governance of other major companies. The Bank will work continually to achieve the best return for related parties, including shareholders, customers, employees and society in general. The efforts to implement the Corporate Governance Guide are the direct responsibility of the Bank's Board of Directors and are consistent with the Central Bank of Libya's publications, regulations and legal requirements. (Al-Nuran Bank website 25/11/2017)

Again, the disclosure is indicative of a stakeholder-oriented approach to corporate governance and an apparent willingness to exceed the minimum legal requirements. A tendency towards mimetic isomorphism (see Section 4.3.2) is also evident in the bank's stated desire to learn from other companies.

Still in the category of board structure and process, Al-Nuran Bank was again unique in describing how directors' remuneration is determined:

> The financial benefits of the Chairman and members of the Board of Directors are determined by resolution of the General Assembly of the Bank, based on a proposal from the Board, in accordance with the recommendations of the Appointment and Remuneration Committee, as set forth in the Bank's corporate governance manual. Members are paid from the date they start attending Board meetings. (Al-Nuran Bank website 25/11/2017)

The disclosure is designed to show that the remuneration policy is shareholder-oriented; the fact that approval is required from the general assembly means that shareholders are able to deploy financial incentives to ensure that executives are aligned with their interests.

In relation to the risk management objectives, system and activities item, the bank explains that

> [t]he Board has set up a comprehensive set of policies covering all local and international bank operations and built a modern risk management system to ensure the continuity of the safety of assets invested. The Bank is dealing with banking risks in an integrated manner and within a comprehensive risk management framework, in accordance with the latest standards, customs and banking practices. This system operates within a multilevel regulatory and control organisational structure to ensure the correct application of the principles of corporate governance. At Board level there are supervisory and control committees to ensure the protection of the assets of the Bank and to apply the concepts of commitment. Other Board committees are concerned with safety and performance improvement at the level of operational activity. (Al-Nuran Bank website 25/11/2017)

The disclosure reflects Al-Nuran Bank's intention to apply best practice in terms of its risk management policy, which it sees as crucial to protect the bank's assets.

Finally, Table 5.13 shows that in 2017, the bank disclosed information on one item in the corporate responsibility and compliance category: its policy and performance in connection with environmental and social responsibility. In this respect, the bank's performance compares with that of the other banks in the sample. Encompassed within its statement of objectives, it explains:

> We aim to build partnerships with all our stakeholders including employees, customers, businesses, suppliers, shareholders – these relationships are the foundation of our business. We will never compromise on our principles or our transparency as these are what make these relationships durable. (Al-Nuran Bank website 25/11/2017)

To conclude, the evidence offered by the bank's website suggests that it has already achieved a good level of corporate governance disclosure and practice, and that it has ambitions to achieve best practice in this area. Interestingly, it is the only bank in the sample to be influenced (or at least, to acknowledge that it is influenced) by the corporate governance practice of other institutions.

5.6 Summary

The first part of the chapter gives some initial indications of the current state of corporate governance disclosure in LCBs. The descriptive analysis of the sample as a whole suggests that the level of corporate governance disclosure provided by commercial banks is low, and that there is no significant variation between banks. The analysis of LCBs' corporate governance disclosure by information category using the ISAR benchmark gives a general picture of current practice and allows some observations about the factors that are shaping this practice. The analysis reveals low rates of corporate governance disclosure when compared to the ISAR benchmark, with 38 of the 52 items not being reported by any of the banks in the sample. Financial and operating results are disclosed by most of the banks, but the only other items that are widely reported (i.e. by at least half of the banks) are ownership structure, changes in shareholdings, company objectives, critical accounting estimates, governance structures such as committees and other mechanisms to prevent conflicts of interest, and policy and performance in connection with environmental and social responsibility.

In the second part of the chapter, the comparison with other developing countries suggests that on average, LCBs exhibit the lowest level of corporate governance disclosure. In most of these countries, the maximum total average level of disclosure across the top ten companies is 9.08 of the ISAR benchmark items, whereas in Libya, the average figure for the top ten commercial banks is 1.58. Interestingly, Libya is even behind countries sharing similar social cultures such as Egypt and Morocco.

The third part of the chapter analyses examples of text published by eleven of the sixteen banks in their annual reports and websites over the period 2007–2017. This section offers initial observations about how corporate governance disclosure has developed and the institutional factors that might be shaping practice in these banks. Table 5.14 summarises the findings of this analysis. Table 5.14 shows that the majority of LCBs appear to be weak in terms of their corporate governance disclosure, though there are individual examples of good practice and evidence of improvement in some banks. The results show that disclosure in most banks is stakeholder-oriented, but that while several banks claim to want to achieve corporate governance best practice, hardly any are willing to go beyond the minimum requirements. There are a number of possible explanations for the current low levels and inferior quality of corporate governance disclosure in LCBs. The main reason may simply be that the concept of corporate governance is still new in the banking sector, and that consequently, key actors lack a true understanding of its importance. This is compounded by the tendency among some to see dedicated corporate governance regulations as redundant because they believe that sufficient provision already exists within Libya's banking and commercial law. The CBL's response to this resistance has arguably been insufficient, both in terms of its efforts at awareness-raising and enforcement, though the dramatic change in Libyan culture and political upheaval since the 2011 revolution may well have impeded its ability and the ability of other institutions to foster real improvement. Progress may also have been slow because there seems at present to be little pressure from either inside or outside stakeholders for the disclosure of non-financial corporate governance information. As long as this remains the case, banks have no immediate reason to consider such information important, and they will continue to give priority to financial results.

Table 5.14: Summary of Evaluation of Annual Reports and Websites.

Name of bank	Evaluation
Jumhoriya Bank	Despite a slight improvement since the launch of the mandatory corporate governance code in 2010, the bank remains weak in terms of corporate governance disclosure. Disclosure is stakeholder-oriented; the examples reveal that the bureaucratic state, as expressed in the CBL, is the main force shaping the bank's corporate governance disclosure and practice. The economic openness programme adopted by the previous regime appears to have had a positive impact, but the dramatic political changes of 2011 have affected this programme and, consequently, Jumhoriya Bank's corporate governance disclosure and practice. The bank seems inclined only to comply with minimum requirements, having started reporting on corporate governance only in 2010 when the corporate governance code became mandatory. Furthermore, its annual reports and web pages cover mandatory items only.
Wahada Bank	This bank discloses information on only a few of the ISAR benchmark items. No significant improvement was observed over the period covered in the annual reports (2007–2010) or that covered in the web pages (2012–2017), despite the bank's claim that it wants to work towards best practice and adopt international standards.
Sahara Bank	The few examples of disclosure that are available for this bank show it is poor at disclosing information about corporate governance. The bank's foreign partner seems to play an essential role in the bank's activities, including its corporate governance.
National Commercial Bank	This bank discloses information on only a few of the ISAR items, though matters have improved slightly since it started reporting about corporate governance on its website in 2012. The bank appears to want to be transparent with its shareholders, providing a dedicated link on its website. It claims that it aims to apply corporate governance best practice and to protect all stakeholders.
United Bank	The bank's disclosure reveals that it aims to achieve international best practice and that it has already exceeded minimum compliance.
Commerce & Development Bank	The bank made some improvement when it began reporting on corporate governance in 2009, but its disclosure is limited. The results reveal that corporate governance in the bank is shaped by the law and by coercive pressure from the CBL. There is no indication that the bank is willing to exceed minimum compliance.
First Gulf Libyan Bank	The corporate governance disclosure is weak, though the bank applies international standards when preparing its financial reports.
Al-Saraya Bank	This bank is weak in terms of corporate governance disclosure, reporting only briefly on governance structures, one board meeting and the background of board members.

Table 5.14 (continued)

Name of bank	Evaluation
North Africa Bank	The corporate governance disclosure is very limited in the bank's annual reports and web pages. Its disclosure regarding the bank's objectives reveals that the bank is seeking to enhance its legitimacy by offering Sharia-based banking.
Al-Amman Bank	The limited corporate governance information on the bank's website reveals that the law is the main factor informing governance in this bank. There is no indication that the bank has any plans to exceed the minimum corporate governance requirements.
Al-Nuran Bank	The textual examples reveal that this bank is applying good corporate governance disclosure and practice. Its disclosure reveals a stakeholder-oriented approach to corporate governance and an ambition to apply best practice. It also shows that this bank is keen to mimic the corporate governance practice of other institutions.

The findings raise a number of questions about the institutional aspects that drive banks to disclose and practise corporate governance, or that deter them from doing so: for example, what makes individual banks disclose information about some aspects of corporate governance and not others? And why do some banks disclose much more than others? It may be helpful to draw on institutional theory to try to answer these questions; to investigate, for example, the influence of isomorphism, how banks respond to this isomorphism, and whether there is any institutional logic behind corporate governance disclosure and practice. The analysis of annual reports and websites alone cannot provide comprehensive answers to these questions; rather, this stage is limited to offering an institutional understanding of corporate governance disclosure and practice and general insights into the current state of this practice in LCBs.

6 Discussion and Conclusion

This is the first study to employ the ISAR benchmark to compare Libya's corporate governance disclosure performance with that of other developing countries. Comparison of corporate governance disclosure in the top ten LCBs with that of the top ten companies in each of 22 other developing countries revealed that LCBs exhibit the lowest level of corporate governance disclosure in their annual reports and websites.

Looking at the picture in the LBS specifically, the report and website analysis revealed low rates of corporate governance disclosure among the sixteen commercial banks in the sector, when compared to the ISAR benchmark. Only fourteen of the 52 items in the index were disclosed, with the most commonly reported items being financial and operating results (by fifteen banks in the sector), company objectives (by fourteen banks), ownership structure (by twelve banks), critical accounting estimates (by twelve banks), policy and performance in connection with environmental and social responsibility (by eleven banks), changes in shareholdings, and governance structures such as committees and other mechanisms to prevent conflicts of interest (by eight banks each). Five banks disclosed information regarding their risk management objectives, system and activities, while three disclosed the qualifications and biographical information of board members. The process for holding annual general meetings, the board's responsibilities regarding financial communications, the composition of the board of directors (executives and non-executives), the determination and composition of directors' remuneration, and mechanisms protecting the rights of other stakeholders in business were disclosed by one bank each. The findings from the textual analysis confirmed that there is a significant lack of corporate governance disclosure in the sector, though there has been some slight improvement, particularly in relation to information about governance structures and corporate governance policy.

When UNCTAD (2011) examined the disclosure practices of the top ten enterprises from each of the 22 emerging economies in the UN, it found that on average, these enterprises reported on two-thirds of the items in the ISAR benchmark. Reporting was more extensive in some of the groups than others; items in the auditing group, for example, were significantly less widely reported than items in the financial transparency group. This was also evident in the current study, with three of the most widely reported items (financial and operating results, company objectives and critical accounting estimates) all being in the financial transparency category, and none of the banks reporting on any of the items in the auditing category. UNCTAD's survey revealed that the majority of disclosure was on mandatory items, though voluntary reporting was also widespread. It concluded that "not surprisingly [...], mandatory items do have a higher rate of disclosure compared with

https://doi.org/10.1515/9783110602111-006

voluntary items" (UNCTAD 2011, p. 14). This is consistent with this study's finding that the few items disclosed by LCBs tend to be mandatory requirements.

On the question of what motivates companies in developing countries to disclose corporate governance information, Oliveira, Ceglia, Lima and Ponte. (2014) found that coercive pressures (i.e. the implementation of laws, rules and sanctions) exert more influence on Brazilian companies than normative pressures (e.g. international organisations' recommendations), but that these coercive pressures actually result in Brazilian companies going beyond what is expected by international bodies such as the UN. The current findings support Oliveira in that they suggest that LCBs disclose information primarily in response to coercive pressure from the CBL, though in the case of the LBS, this coercive pressure is much more limited both in its ambition and its impact.

As the findings from analysis of annual reports and websites indicates, although Egypt is slightly ahead of Libya in terms of its corporate governance disclosure performance, it still sits near the bottom of UNCTAD's league table. This is confirmed in another study by UNCTAD (2007), which identifies low rates of corporate governance disclosure among Egypt's CASE 30 enterprises when compared to the ISAR benchmark. There are some similarities between the findings of the current study and UNCTAD's findings for Egypt; in both countries, financial and operating results, company objectives and critical accounting estimates are widely reported. However, UNCTAD found that in Egypt, the nature, type and elements of related party transactions, and risk management objectives, system and activities are also widely disclosed. Another, more recent, Egypt-based study by Samaha, Dahawy, Hussainey and Stapleton. (2012) also found generally minimal levels of corporate governance in the country's listed companies, though it identified high levels of disclosure for those items that are mandatory under the EAS.

The findings of the empirical analysis provide information regarding the recent development of corporate governance disclosure in LCBs, thereby narrowing the literature gap in relation to corporate governance disclosure in banks in general (Darmadi 2013; Feldioreanu and Seriaa 2015; Nwakama, Okereke and Arewa 2011; Thomas and Boolaky 2009) and in the MENA countries in particular (Union of Arab Banks 2007). It is the first study to give insights into the level of corporate governance disclosure being offered by Libyan banks, thereby allowing comparison with corporate governance disclosure levels in other developing and developed countries.

The study is especially useful because it adopts an empiric approach, gathering evidence from banks' annual reports and websites to assess the level of corporate governance disclosure against national and international requirements. It enriches our knowledge by providing examples of this disclosure and showing both its quality and scope; in this way, it is able to shed light on which aspects of corporate governance LCBs consider worth prioritizing, and where, if anywhere, there has been improvement.

The findings provide up-to-date evidence about the recent development of corporate governance practice in LCBs. This is especially important, given the seismic changes that have taken place in the Libyan environment since previous studies were conducted. The years since 2011 have seen major corporate governance reforms introduced within the banking sector, but more than this, they have witnessed dramatic cultural and political changes across Libya as a whole. This study offers crucial evidence of how LCBs are being affected by these changes, and how they are responding to these reforms.

When the findings are considered from the perspective of institutional theory, the first conclusion that may be drawn is that its assumptions regarding institutional isomorphism do not seem to hold true in the Libyan environment. The findings suggest that commercial banks in the LBS have not, on the whole, felt compelled to adapt themselves or their practice in response to coercive, normative or mimetic pressures. For example, the coercive pressure being exerted by the CBL, although the main institutional force driving banks to implement corporate governance, has been insufficient to properly institutionalise corporate governance disclosure in the LBS; even though the corporate governance code has been mandatory since 2010, disclosure remains very weak in all banks. Normative pressures have had even less impact on banks' behaviour, with most banks failing to respond to the international standards for corporate governance disclosure issued by bodies such as the BCBS and the OECD. There does not appear to be any normative pressure from national organisations such as the LAAA or Libya's banking bodies. The only banks to exhibit any tendency towards mimetic isomorphism have been those with foreign partners, and they appear to be motivated mainly by uncertainty, mimicking the practice of their foreign partner because they are unsure about corporate governance. It can thus be concluded that institutional pressures in the LBS produce different results from those seen in developed and even other developing countries.

6.1 Practical Implications

The analysis reveals that despite the CBL's efforts to improve corporate governance in the banking sector, first through the voluntary CGLBS (2006) and then through the mandatory CGLBS (2010), there remains a significant lack of disclosure.

The implication of the findings seems to be that the CBL needs to be much stricter in enforcing compliance from those banks that are failing to reach even the minimum requirements of corporate governance disclosure, for example by imposing penalties and fines. At the same time, it should also focus more on its cooperative role with these banks and expand its efforts to raise awareness of corporate governance through workshops, conferences and training courses for BMs, EMs, regulators and those responsible for preparing annual reports. In banks that limit their compliance to the minimum requirements, the CBL should focus on the causes of this behaviour. For example, if the bank does no more than it has to because it regards corporate governance as merely an externally imposed set of restrictions, the CBL should seek to raise awareness about the potential benefits of implementing corporate governance. Education is also important in the case of banks that are exceeding the minimum requirements; if they are imitating their foreign partner because they are uncertain about what they should be doing, the CBL has a role to play in helping them understand the point of applying corporate governance in their bank and clarifying their objectives.

6.2 Limitations and Future Research Opportunities

There are some important limitations to the study that need to be taken into account when considering its findings. One important limitation is that in the analysis of the annual reports and websites of the study, difficulties in accessing the annual reports for some banks meant that it was not always possible to include the most recent annual report. Similarly, while the Wayback Machine website allowed the collection of website data over several years, making it possible to see the historical improvement in online corporate governance disclosure right up to the present day, some pages were inevitably missed. The fact that annual reports and websites present different data in different ways makes comparison between the banks more difficult, but the findings of the textual analysis were also limited by virtue of the fact that information was available on only a few aspects of corporate governance (i.e. changes in shareholdings, ownership structure, bank objectives, governance structures such as committees and other mechanisms to prevent conflicts of interest, and risk management objectives).

There are very few studies investigating corporate governance in Libya, so there are a number of ways in which the gap in the literature might be reduced. For example, this book focuses on the banking sector, but the investigation should be extended to other industries to provide a clearer picture of how Libyan companies are responding to national and international corporate governance requirements.

Previous studies have tended to use annual reports as their main source of data; to the best of the author's knowledge, this is the first Libya-based study to draw some of its data from websites. Since the findings suggest that this is a fruitful source of disclosure-related data, other researchers might also find it helpful to use websites to investigate both financial and non-financial disclosure in the banking sector and beyond.

The results of the study show that there has been a slight improvement in corporate governance disclosure since 2010, with more banks starting to provide information about their corporate governance practice in their annual reports and websites. Other researchers might continue the work started here by taking advantage of this disclosure to investigate banks' corporate governance practice and the factors that affect this practice. Another suggestion is for researchers to pay closer attention to specific aspects of corporate governance, such as the practice and disclosure surrounding board remuneration policy. Finally, this study was conducted in a single MENA country. Further research is needed to increase understanding of the development of corporate governance disclosure and practice in other societies.

References

Abdeen, A. (1989). *English-Arabic Dictionary of Accounting and Financial*. John Wiley Sons, London.

ABDUSSALAM, A. A., (1985). The impact of recent economic changes in Libya on monetary aggregates. In: BURU, M.M., GHANEM, S.M., and MCLACHLAN, K.S., (eds.). Planning and development in modern Libya. UK, Middle East and North African Studies press, 77–90.

Abida, S. R. (2011). *The Impact of the World Trade Orgnisation on Libyan Banking Sector*. Liverpool, United Kingdom: Liverpool John Moores Univesity.

Abouzkeh, A. (2013). *A Critical Perspective on Social Accounting in Banking : " The Case of Social Accounting in the Libyan Commercial Banking Sector."* (doctoral dissertation) Dundee, Scotland: University of Dundee.

Abubaker, A. (2007). Influence of core cultural values on the communication behaviour of staff in Libyan organisation. Research Paper, Annual Review of Education, Communication and Language Science, ARECLS, 4.

Abu-Tapanjeh, A. M. (2009). Corporate governance from the Islamic perspective: A comparative analysis with OECD principles. Critical Perspectives on Accounting, 20(5), 556–567.

Aghila, E. (2000). *Job satisfaction and work commitment in the context of Libya*. (Doctoral dissertation). Manchester, England: Manchester Metropolitan University.

Agnaia, A. (1997). Management Training and Development within its Environment: The Case of Libyan Industrial Companies. *International Journal of European Industrial Training, 21, No. 3*, 117–123.

Agrawal, A., and Knoeber, C. R. (1996). Firm Performance and Mechanisms to Control Agency Problems between Managers and Shareholders. *The Journal of Financial and Quantitative Analysis, 31 (3)*, 377–397.

Agyris, C. (1973). Some Limits of Rational Man Organisational Theory". *Public Administration Review, 33*, 253–267.

Ahmad, N. S., and Gao, S. S. (2004). Changes, problems and challenges of accounting education in Libya. *Accounting Education, 13*(3), 365–390.

Alexander, J. (1983). *Theoretical Logic in Sociology. Vols. 1–4. Berkeley: University of California Press.*

Allen, F. (2005). Corporate governance in emerging economies. *Oxford Review of Economic Policy, 21*(2), 164–177.

Al-Malkawi, H. A. N., Pillai, R., & Bhatti, M. I. (2014). Corporate governance practices in emerging markets: The case of GCC countries. *Economic Modelling*, 38, 133–141. http://doi.org/10.1016/j.econmod.2013.12.019

Al-Moataz, E., and Hussainey, K. (2012). Determinants of corporate governance disclosure in Saudi companies. *Journal of Economics and Management, 1*, 1–24.

Aoki, M. (1996). Towards a comparative institutional analysis: Motivations and some tentative theorizing'. *Japanese Economic Review, 47 (1)*, 1–19.

Arafa, I. (2012). *Evaluating the impact of institutional logic on the corporate Internet reporting by Egyptian listed companies*. (doctoral dissertation), Birmingham, England: Aston University.

Arcot, S. R., and Brun, V. G. (2006). In Letter but not in Spirit: An Analysis of Corporate Governance in the UK. Unpublished Working Paper, Available at: http://ssm.com/abstract.

Arcot, S. R., and Brun, V. G. (2006).around the world'. Journal of Finance, vol. 54, no. 2, pp. 471–517.

Arun, T. G., and Turner, J. (2004). Corporate Governance of Banks in Developing Economies: concepts and issues. *Corporate Governance: An International Review, 12(3)*, 371–377.

Asad, T. (2009). *Genealogies of religion: Discipline and reasons of power in Christianity and Islam*. Baltimore and London: JHU Press.

Attir Moa, and Al-Azzabi, K (2004). *The Libyan Jamahiriya: Country, People, Social and Political Development. Doing business with Libya*. London, UK: Kogan Page Ltd.

https://doi.org/10.1515/9783110602111-007

Ayuso, S., Rodríguez, M. A., García-Castro, R., and Ariño, M. A. (2014). Maximizing stakeholders' interests: An empirical analysis of the stakeholder approach to corporate governance. Business and society, 53(3), 414–439.

Bait El-Mal, M., Smith, C., and Taylor, M. (1973): The Development of Accounting in Libya,. *The International Journal of Accounting, Education and Research, 8 (2)*, 83–101.

Bait El-Mal, M., Smith, C., and Taylor, M. (1973): Banking Organisation.' Basel, Switzerland.: Bank for International Settlement.

Bareney, J. B. (1990). The Debate Between Traditional Management Theory And Orgnisational Economics: Substantive Differences or Inter Group Conflict. *The Academy of Mangement Review, 15 (3)*, 382–393.

Barley, S. R., and Tolbert, P. S. (1997). Institutionalization and structuration: Studying the links between action and institution. Organisation studies, *18(1)*, 93–117.

Basel Committee on Banking Supervision 2006. 'Enhancing Corporate Governance for

Becht, M., Bolton, P.,and Roell, A. (2003). Corporate governance and control. In *Handbook of the Economics of Finance* (Vol.1, pp. 1–109).

Beekes, W., and Brown, P. (2006). Do Better-Governed Australian Firms Make More Informative Disclosures?. Journal of Business Finance and Accounting, 33(3–4), 422–450.

Bengdara, F. (2007). Improving and Restructuring commercial banks Libyan banks. Tripoli, Libya: CBL Central bank of Libya.

Betty, B., and Zajac, E. (1994). Managerial incentives, monitoring and risk of executive compensation, ownership and board structure in initial public offering. *Administrative Science Quarterly*, 39(2),313–335.

Bill, J., and Hardgrave, R. (1981). *Comparative Politics: The Quest for Theory. Columbus, Ohio: Merrill.*

Bricker, R., & Chandar, C. (1998). On applying agency theory in historical accounting research. *Business and Economic History, 27(2)*, 486–498.

Bourdieu, P., and Farage, S. (1994). Rethinking the state: Genesis and structure of the bureaucratic field. Sociological theory, 12(1),1–18.

Bukhari, M. S. (2014). *The impact of institutions on the development of corporate governance in Saudi Arabia.* (Doctoral dissertation), Nottingham, England: University of Nottingham.

Burgess, J. (1902). *Political Science and Comparative Constitutional Law. Boston: Ginn.*

Burns, J., and Scapens, R. W. (2000). Conceptualizing management accounting change: an institutional framework. *Management Accounting Research, 11*, 3–25.

Bushman, R., Chen, Q., Engel, E., and Smith, A. (2004). Financial accounting information, organisational complexity and corporate governance systems. *Journal of Accounting and Economics*, 37(2), 167–201.

Caprio Jr., G. and R. Levine (2002), "Corporate Governance in Finance: Concepts and International Observations" in Financial Sector Governance: The Roles of the Public and Private Sectors, Eds. R.E. Litan, M. Pomerleano, and V. Sundararajan, Washington DC: The Brookings Institution, 17–50.

CBL. (2006). *Central Bank of Libya. Fiftieth anniversary of the founding 1956–2006. Researches and Statistics Department in CBL.* Retrieved from https://cbl.gov.ly

CBL. (2009). Economic Database. The evolution of the most important business indicators of Commercial Banks Until the third quarter, Tripoli, Libya: Tipoly.

CPI (2010) Corruption Perceptions Index, Transparency International Available on: https://www.transparency.org/research/cpi/cpi_2009/0#results

CBL. (2010a). *Central Bank of Libya. The third annual report for manage the monitory on banks and monetary for years 2010 and 2011.*

CBL. (2010b). *Central Bank of Libya. The improvement in monetary policy and banking in Libya. The Regular session of thirty four for board of governors and Arabic monetary institutions in Tripoli.. CBL.*

CBL. (2012). *The fourth annual report*. Tripoli, Libya: Cental Bank of LIBYA.
corporate governanceLBS. (2006). Corporate Governance: Guideline for Board of Directors of Libyan Banks. Central Bank of Libya. Tripoli, Libya: Tripoly.
corporate governanceLBS. (2010). The corporate governance code of the libyan banking sector. Libyan Central Bank. Tripoli. Retrieved from: http://www.lsm.ly/LSM_Investor_Releases1/AssBook.pdf
corporate governanceLSM. (2007). *CGLSM Corporate governance code libyan stoke market. Libyan Stoke Market LSM.*
Chami, R., Al-Darwish, A., Cevik, S., Charap, J., George, S., Gracia, Gracia, B. and Pattanayak, S. (2012). Libya beyond the revolution: challenges and opportunities.
Chang, H.-J. (2002). Breaking the Mould: An Institutionalist Political Economy Alternative to the Neoliberal Theory of the Market and the State. *Cambridge Journal of Economics*, *26*(5), 539–559.
Che, J., and Qian, Y. (1998). Institutional environment, community government, and corporate governance: Understanding China's township-village enterprises. *Journal of Law, Economics, and Organisation*, vol. 14(1), 1–23.
Cioffi, J. W. (2000). Governing Globalization? The State, Law, and Structural Change in Corporate Governance. *Journal of Law and Society*, *27*(4), 572–600.
CIPE. (2003). Corporate governance in Morocco, Egypt, Lebanon, and Jordan. The Center for International Private Enterprise 2012 E. Retrieved from: https://www.cipe.org/
Claessens, S., and Laeven, L. (2006). International Corporate Finance, the world bank, 1, 1–418.
Claessens, S., and Yurtoglu, B. B. (2013). Corporate governance in emerging markets A survey. *Emerging Markets Review*, *15*, 1–33.
Clarke, T. (2004). Cycles of Crisis and Regulation: the enduring agency and stewardship problems of corporate governance. Corporate Governance. *An International Review*, *12(2)*, 153–161.
Clement, R. W. (2005). The Lessons from Stakeholder Theory for U. S. Business Leaders. *Business Horizons*, *48*, 255–264.
Committee to Protect Journalists. (2007). *Attacks on the Press: Middle East and North Africa Snapshots*. Retrieved from https://cpj.org/2008/02/attacks-on-the-press-2007-snapshotsattacks-develop-2.php
Commons, J. (1924). *The Legal Foundations of Capitalism*. New York: Macmillan.
Cooke, T. E. (1992). The impact of size, stock market listing and industry type on disclosure in the annual reports of Japanese listed corporations. *Accounting and business research*, 22(87), 229–237.
Council, F. R. (2010). The UK corporate governance code. London: Financial Reporting Council.
Daily, C. M., Dalton, D. R., & Canella, A. A. (2003). Corporate Governance: Decades of Dialogue and Data. *Academy of Management Review*, 28(3), 371–382.
Darmadi, S. (2013). Corporate governance disclosure in the annual report: An exploratory study on Indonesian Islamic banks. *Humanomics*, *29*(1), 4–23.
Davie, G. (2006). Sociology of religion. In *The Blackwell companion to the study of religion* (pp. 43, 171).
Davis, J., Schoorman, F., and Donaldson, L. (1997). Stewardship Theory of Management. *Academy of Management Review*, *22 (1)*, 20–47.
Deegan, C., and Unerman, J. (2006). *Financial accounting theory*. London: Mcorporate governanceraw-Hill.
Deephouse, D. L.. (1996). Does Isomorphism Legitimate? *The Academy of Management Journal*, *39*(4), 1024–1039.
Dela Rama, M. (2012). Corporate governance and corruption: Ethical dilemmas of Asian business groups. *Journal of Business Ethics*, *109(4)*, 501–519.
Democracy reporting international. (2016). *Electoral Provisions in Libyan draft Constitution*.

DiMaggio, P. J., and Powell, W. W. (1983). The Iron Cage Revisited: Institutional Isomorphism and Collective Rationality in Organisational Fields. *American Sociological Review, 48 (2)*, 147–60.

Dittmar, A., Mahrt-Smith, J., and Servaes, H. (2003). International corporate governance and corporate cash holdings. *Journal of Financial and Quantitative Analysis, 38 (1)*, 111–134.

Donaldson, L. (1990b). The ethereal hand: Organisational economics and management theory. *Academy of management* Review, 15(3), 369–381.

Donaldson, L., and Davis, J. H. (1991). Stewardship theory or agency theory: CEO governance and shareholder returns. *Australian Journal of management*, 16(1), 49–64.

Donaldson, T., and Preston, L. E. (1995). The stakeholder theory of the corporation: Concepts, evidence, and implications. *Academy of management Review*, 20(1), 65–91.

Donaldson. (1990a). A rational basis for criticisms of organisational economics: A reply to Barney. *Academy of Management Review*, 15(3), 394–401.

Dore, R. (1983). Goodwill and the spirit of market capitalism. *British Journal of Sociology, 34*, 459–482.

Dragomir, V.-D. (2008). Highlights for a History of Corporate Governance. *European Journal of Management.* Available at SSRN: https://ssrn.com/abstract=1114045.

Dulewicz, V. A. H., P. (2004). Does the Composition and Practice of Boards of Directors Bear Any Relationship to the performance of their Companies? *Corporate Governance: An International Review, 12(3)*, 263–280.

Dunn, M. B., and Jones, C. (2010). Institutional Logics and Institutional Pluralism: The Contestation of Care and Science Logics in Medical Education, 1967–2005. *Administrative Science Quarterly, 55*(1), 114–149.

Durkheim, E. (1893/1949) The Division of Labor in Society. Glencoe, IL: Free Press.

Elkington, J. (2004). *Enter the Triple Bottom Line.* In Henriques, A., Richardson, J. (Ed.) The Triple Bottom Line, Does It All Add Up? Assessing The Sustainability of Business and CSR. Earthscan, London.

Ellabbar, K. (2007). *Capital market and accounting disclosure in emerging economies: The case of Libya.* (Doctoral Dissertation) Greater Manchester, England: University of Salford.

Everett, J. (2002). Organisational research and the praxeology of Pierre Bourdieu. *Organisational Research Methods, 5(1)*, 56–80.

Ezzamel, M., and Willmott, H. (1993). Corporate governance and financial accountability: Recent reforms in the UK public sector. *Accounting Auditing and Accountability Journal, 6 (3)*, 109–132.

Feldioreanu, I. A., and Seriaa, C. (2015). Corporate governance disclosure of banks in Romania and Malaysia and the quality of the web sites. *Corporate governance*, 14(1),193–216.

Feldman, M., and Rafaeli, A. (2002). Organisational routines as sources of connections and understandings. *'Journal of Management Studies, (39)*, 309–331.

Filatotchev, I., Lien, Y. C., and Piesse, J. (2005). Corporate Governance and Performance in Publicly Listed, Family-Controlled Firms : Evidence from Taiwan. *Journal of Management, 22(3), 257.*

Filatotchev, I., Lien, Y. C., and Piesse, J. finance'. *Journal of Political Economy*, 106, 1113–1155.

Fiss, P. C., and Zajac, E. J. (2004). The diffusion of ideas over contested terrain: The (non)adoption of a shareholder value orientation among German firms. Administrative Science Quarterly, 49 (4), 501–534.

Fiss, P. C., and Zajac, E. J. (2006). The symbolic management of strategic change: Sensegiving via framing and decoupling. *Academy of Management Journal, 49*(6), 1173–1193.

Fiss, P. C. 2008. Institutions and corporate governance. In R. Greenwood, C. Oliver, K. Sahlin, & R. Suddaby (Eds.), The Sage handbook of organizational institutionalism: 389–410. London: Sage.

Fligstein, N. (1996). Markets as politics: A political-cultural approach to market institutions. *American Sociological Review, 61(4)*, 656–673.

Fligstein, N., and Mara-Drita, I. (1996). How to make a market: Reflections on the attempt to create a single market in the European Union. *American Journal of Sociology, 102*(1), 1–33.
Freeman, R. (1984). Strategic Management: A Stakeholder Approach, Pitman, Boston
Freeman, R. E., & McVea, J. 2001. A stakeholder approach to strategic management. In M. A. Hitt, R. E. Freeman, & J. S. Harrison (Eds.), Handbook of strategic management: 189–207. Oxford, UK: Blackwell.
Friedland, R., and Alford, R. R. (1991). *Bringing society back in: Symbols, practices and institutional contradictions. The New Institutionalism in Organisational Analysis*. Chicago: University of Chicago Press.
Fung, B. (2014). The demand and need for transparency and disclosure in corporate governance. *Universal Journal of Management*, 2(2), 72–80.
GAN. (2016). business anti corruption. Libya Corruption Report, available at www.business-anti-corruption.com/country-profiles/libya.
Germain, L., Galy, N., and Lee, W. (2014). Corporate governance reform in Malaysia: Board size, independence and monitoring. Journal of Economics and Business, 75, 126–162.
Ghoshal, S., and Moran, P. (1996). Bad for practice: A critique of the transaction cost theory. *Academy of management Review*, 21(1), 13–47.
Gibbins, M., Richardson, A., & Waterhouse, J. (1990). The management of corporate financial disclosure: opportunism, ritualism, policies, and processes. *Journal of Accounting Research*, 28(1), 121–143.
Gibbs, J. P. (1965). Norms: The problem of definition and classification. *American Journal of Sociology, 70*(5), 586–594.
Gillan, S., and Starks, L. T. (1998). A Survey of Shareholder Activism: Motivation and Empirical Evidence. *Contemporary Finance Digest, 2*(3), 10–34. http://doi.org/10.2139/ssrn.663523.
Granovetter, M. (1985). Economic action and social structure: The problem of embeddedness. *American Journal of Sociology, 91*, 481–510.
Grecco, M. C. P., FM Filho, M. A., Segura, L. C., Sanchez, I. M. G., and Dominguez, L. R. (2013). The voluntary disclosure of sustainable information: a comparative analysis of spanish and brazilian companies. Journal of Accounting and Organisations, 17, 45–55.
Greenwood, R., & Hinings, C. R. (1996). Understanding Radical Organisational Change: Bringing together the Old and the New Institutionalism Authors. *The Academy of Management Review, 21(4)*, 1022–1054.
Greenwood, R., Raynard, M., Kodeih, F., Micelotta, E. R., and Lounsbury, M. (2011). Institutional Complexity and Organisational Responses. *The Academy of Management Annals, 5*(1), 317–371.
Greenwood, R., Suddaby, R., and Hinings, C. (2002). Theorizing Change : the Role of Professional Associations in the Transformation of. *Academy of Management Journal, 45*(1), 58–80.
Groves, T., Hong, Y., McMillan, J., and Naughton, B. (1995). China's evolving managerial labor market. *Journal of Political Economy, 103(4)*, 873–892.
Gup, Benton, 2007, "Corporate Governance in Banks: Does the Board Structure Matter," in Corporate Governance in Banking, (Benton Gup, ed.), Edward Elgar, Cambridge, Cheltenham, UK, pp. 18–39.
Hall, P. A., and Thelen, K. (2009). Institutional change in varieties of capitalism. *Socio-economic review*, 7(1), 7–34.
Hampel Committee. (1998). Final Report of the Committee on Corporate Governance. Gee, London), (The 1998 Code). ICAEW.
Harrison, G., and McKinnon, J. (1986). Culture and accounting change: A new perspective on corporate reporting regulation and accounting policy formulation, *Accounting, Organisations and Society, 11(3)*, 233–52.

Hart, O. (1995). Corporate governance: Some theory and implication. *Economic Journal, 105 (430)*, 678–689.
Hawashe, A. (2014). *An evaluation of voluntary disclosure in the annual report of commercial banks: Empirical evidence from libya.* (Doctoral dissertation) Greater Manchester, England: University of Salford.
Hawkamah, and IFC. (2008). A Corporate Governance Survey of Listed Companies and Banks A Cross the Middle East and North Africa. International Finance Corporation, and Hawkamah-The Institute for Corporate Governance. Reverted from: www.ifc.org
Hendriksen, E. S. (1970). Accounting Theory. Rev. ed. Homewood, Illinois: Richard D. Irwin.
Hendriksen, E. S. (1982). *Accounting Theory. Homewood,* Illinois, USA: *Richard D.Irwin, Inc.*
Hill, C. W., and Jones, T. M. (1992). Stakeholder-agency theory. *Journal of Management Studies, 29(2)*, 131–154.
Hoffman, A. (1999). Institutional evolution and change: Environmentalism and the US chemical industry'. Academy of Management Journal, 42 (4), 351–371.
Hoffman, A., and Wooten, M. (2008). Organisational Fields: Past, present and future. In R. Greenwood, C. Oliver, K. Sahlim, R. Suddaby, *The Sage Handbook of Organisational Institutionalism* (pp. 130–148). London: Sage Publications.
Hofstede, G. (1980). *Culture's Consequences: International Differences in Work- Related Values,*. London: Sage.
Hofstede, G. (1984). Cultural dimensions in management and planning. Asia Pacific journal of management, 1(2), 81–99.
Holmstrom, B., and Kaplan, S. N. (2003). The state of US corporate governance: what's right and what's wrong?. Journal of Applied Corporate Finance, 15(3), 8–20.
Hopt, K. J., and Leyens, P. C. (2004). Board models in Europe–recent developments of internal corporate governance structures in Germany, the United Kingdom, France, and Italy. *European Company and Financial Law Review*, 1(2), 135–168.
Huntington, S. P. (1968). Political order in changing societies, New Haven: Yale University Press London.
Husien, N., and Havard, T. (1990). The Role of the Banking Sector in Increasing the Efficiency of the Fishing Industry in Libya, University of Salford, Greater Manchester, England. 175–183.
IFC. (2015). Corporate Governance: Middle East and North Africa. Washington, USA: International Finance Corporation.
ISAR. (2011). Corporate Governance Disclosure in Emerging Markets. UNITED NATIONS. New York and Geneva.
Ittonen, K., 2010. A Theoretical Examination of the Role of Auditing and the Relevance of Audit Reports, VAASA, pp. 61.
Jensen, M. C., & Meckling, W. H. (1976). Theory of the firm: Managerial behavior, agency costs and ownership structure. Journal of financial economics, 3(4), 305–360.
Jensen, M. C. (1994). Self-interest, altruism, incentives, and agency theory. Journal of applied corporate finance, 7(2), 40–45.
Jepperson, R. (1991). Institutions, institutional effects, and institutionalism. *The New Institutionalism in Organisational Analysis, 6*, 143–163.
Jiang, Y., and Peng, M. W. (2011). Are family ownership and control in large firms good, bad, or irrelevant? *Asia Pacific Journal of Management, 28*(1), 15–39.
Keasey, K., Thompson, S., and Wright, M. (1997). *Corporate Governance: Economic and Financial Issues*. Oxford: Oxford University Press.
Keasey, K., Thompson, S., and Wright, M. (Eds.). (2005). Corporate governance: accountability, enterprise and international comparisons. West Sussex, England: John Wiley and Sons.

Khadaroo, I., and Shaikh, J. M. (2007). Corporate governance reforms in Malaysia: insights from institutional theory. World Review of Entrepreneurship, Management and Sustainable Development, 3(1), 37.

Khadaroo, I., and Shaikh, J. M. (2007). Corporate governance reforms in Malaysia: insights from institutional theory. *World Review of Entrepreneurship, Management and Sustainable Development, 3*(1), 37.

Kilani, A. (1988). *The Evolution and Status of Accounting in Libya.* Hull, England: (Doctoral Dissertation) Hull University.

Kim, E. (1991). "The Industrial Organisation and Growth of the Korean Chaebol", in Hamilton, G. (ed) Business Networks and Economic Development in East and Southeast Asia, Hong Kong: Centre of Asian Studies, University of Hong Kong.

Kim, E. H. (1998). Globalization of capital markets and the Asian financial crisis. Journal of Applied Corporate Finance, 11(3), 30–39.

Krenn, M. (2014). Decoupling as a Sustainable Firm Response to Pressures for Convergence and Divergence in Corporate Governance: The Case of Codes of Good Corporate Governance. *Journal of Management Policy and Practice, 15*(4), 103–117.

Kribat, M. (2009). *Financial disclosure practices in developing countries: evidence from the Libyan banking sector.* Dundee, Scotland: (Doctoral Dissertation) University of Dundee.

La Porta, R., Lopez-de-Silanes, F., and Shleifer, A. (1999) 'Corporate ownership

La Porta, R., Lopez-de-Silanes, F., Shleifer, A., and and Vishny, R. (1997). Legal determinants of external finance'. *Journal of Finance, 52*, 1131–1150.

La Porta, R., Lopez-de-Silanes, F., Shleifer, A., and Vishny, R. (2000). Investor protection and corporate governance. *Journal of Financial Economics, 58(1)*, 3–27.

La Porta, R., Lopez-de-Silanes, F., Shleifer, A., and Vishny, R. (1998) 'Law and

La Torre, M. (2010) Law as Institution. Law and Philosophy Library Series, (vol. 90). Heidelberg: Springer.

Larbsh, M. M. (2010). *An Evaluation of Corporate Governance Practice in Libya : Stakeholders' Perspectives.* Nottingham, England: (Doctoral dissertation) The Nottingham Trent University.

Learmount, S. (2003). Theorizing corporate governance: organizational alternatives. Journal of Interdisciplinary Economics, 14(2), 159–173.

Letza, S., Kirkbride, J., Sun, X., & Smallman, C. (2008). Corporate Governance Theorising: Limits, Critics And Alternatives. *International Journal of Law and Management*, 50(1), 17–32.

Letza, S., Sun, X., and Kirkbride, J. (2004). Shareholding versus stakeholding: A critical review of corporate governance. *Corporate Governance: An International Review*, 12(3), 242–262.

Levine, R. (2004). *The corporate governance of banks: A concise discussion of concepts and evidence* (Vol. 3404). Washington, D.C: World Bank Publications.

Lin, C. (2001). Corporatisation and corporate governance in China's economic transition. *Journal of Economics Literature, 34 (1–2)*, 5–35.

Litvak, K. (2007). The effect of the Sarbanes-Oxley Act on non-US companies cross-listed in the US. *Journal of Corporate Finance, 13*, 195–228.

Lu, C.-L., and Chen, T. C. (2009). A study of applying data mining approach to the information disclosure for Taiwan's stock market investors. *Expert Systems with Applications, 36*(2), 3536–3542. http://doi.org/10.1016/j.eswa.2008.02.007

Lundgren, M., and Catasús, B. (2000). The banks' impact on the natural environment – on the space between "what is" and "what if." Business Strategy and the Environment, 9(3), 186–195.

Luoma, P., & Goodstein, J. (1999). Stakeholders and corporate boards: Institutional influences on board composition and structure. *Academy of management journal*, 42(5), 553–563.

Madhani, P. M. (2015). Corporate governance and disclosure practices of MNC subsidiaries and cross-listed firms: An institutional environment perspective. Browser Download This Paper.

Magrus, A. (2012). *Corporate Governance Practices in Developing Countries: The Case of Libya.* Gloucestershire, UK: (Doctoral dissertation, University of Gloucestershire).

Maingot, M. and Zeghal, D. (2008) „An analysis of corporate governance information disclosure by Canadian banks", *Corporate Ownership and Control*, vol. 5, no. 2: 225–236

Mallin, C. A. (2007). *Corporate Governance (2 ed.).* New York: Oxford University Press.

March, J. and Olsen, J. (1996). Institutional perspectives on political institutions. *Governance, 9(3),* 247–264.

March, J., and Olsen, J. (1984). "The new institutionalism: Organisational factors in political life". *The American Political Science Review*, 78, 734–749.

March, J., and Olsen, J. (1989). Rediscovering Institutions: The Organisational Basis of Politics. New York: Free Press.

Maw, N. G., Lane of HorseH, P. S. L. B., Craig-Cooper, S. M. and Alsbury, A. 1994. Maw on corporate governance. Aldershot: Dartmouth.

Mayer, K., and Solomon, R. (2006). Capabilities, contractual hazards, and governance: Integrating resource-based and transaction cost perspectives. *Academy of Management Journal, 49 (5),* 942–959.

Meyer, J. W., and Rowan, B. (1977). Institutionalized organisations: Formal structure as myth and ceremony. American Journal of Sociology, 83(2), 340–363.

Milhaupt, C. J. (1996). A relational theory of Japanese corporate governance: contract, culture, and the rule of law. *Harvard International Law Journal, 37*, 3–64.

Mitton, T. (2002). A cross-firm analysis of the impact of corporate governance on the East Asian financial crisis. Journal of Financial Economics, 64(2), 215–241.

Moll, J., Burns, J., and Major, M. (2006). 'Institutional theory', in Z. Hoque (ed.), Methodological issues in accounting research: Theories and methods, Spiramus, London, UK, pp. 183–205.

Monks, R., and Minow, N. (2008). *Corporate Governance* (4 ed). Oxford, United kingdom: Wiley and Sons, Ltd.

Moyo, T., & Rohan, S. (2006). Corporate citizenship in the context of the financial services sector: what lessons from the Financial Sector Charter?. Development Southern Africa, 23(2), 289–303.

North, D. C. (1990). *Institutions, Institutional Change and Economic Performance.* Cambridge, Cambridge University Press.

Nwakama, P. C., Okereke, E. J., and Arewa, A. (2011). An empirical evaluation of corporate governance mechanism in banking sector: impact and implication in Nigeria. *Asian Journal of Business and Management Sciences*, 1(2), 202–236.

OBG. (2008). *The Report: Libya.* Oxford Business Group. Oxford.

OECD. (2004). *Principles of Corporate Governance 2004.* Organisation for economic co-operation and development. (Vol. 13). 1–178.

Oliveira, M., Ceglia, D., Lima, L., and Ponte, V. (2014). Analysis of Corporate Governance Disclosure in the Light of Institutional Theory: a Study on Brazilian Companies, 1–16. Available via http://www.anpad.org.br/admin/pdf/2014_EnANPAD_CON1530.pdf

Osama, M. B. M. (2013). *Transparency and Disclosure, Company Characteristics and Financial Performance : A Study of the Emerging Libyan Stock Market.* Huddersfield, England: (doctoral dissertation), University of Huddersfield.

Othman, H. Ben, and Zeghal, D. (2010). Investigating transparency and disclosure determinants at firm-level in MENA emerging markets. *International Journal of Accounting, Auditing and Performance Evaluation*, *6*(4), 368.

Pande, S., and Ansari, V. A. (2014). A theoretical framework for corporate governance. Indian Journal of Corporate Governance, 7(1), 56–72.

Parsons, T. (1934/1990) 'Prolegomena to a theory of social institutions'. American Sociological Review, vol. 55, pp. 319–339.

Parsons, T. (1991). *The Social System*. Glellcoe: Free Press.
Patel, S. A., Balic, A., and Bwakira, L. (2002). Measuring transparency and disclosure at firm- level in emerging markets. *Emerging Markets Review, 3*, 325–337. http://doi.org/10.1016/S1566-0141(02)00040-7
Peng, M. W. (2003). Institutional Transitions and Strategic Choices. *Academy of Management Review, 28*(2), 275–296.
Peng, M. W., and Heath, P. S. (1996). The growth of the firm in planned economies in transition: Institution, and strategic choice. *Academy of Management Review, 21*(2), 492–528.
Perrow, C. (1986). Complex Organisations: A Critical Essay. New York: Mcorporate governanceraw- Hill.
Powell, W., and DiMaggio, P. (Eds.). (1991). *The New Institutionalism in Organisational Analysis*. Chicago: University of Chicago Press.
Porter, M., and Yegin, D. (2006). "National economic strategy: an assessment of the competitiveness of the Libyan Arab Jamahiriya". The general planning council of Libya. Cera, UK.
Pratten, J. and Mashat, A. (2009). Corporate Social Disclosure in Libya. *Social Responsibility Journal, 5, No. 3*, 311–327.
Qu, W., and Leung, P. (2006). Cultural impact on Chinese corporate disclosure–a corporate governance perspective. *Managerial Auditing Journal*, 21(3), 241–264.
Radcliffe-Brown, A. R. (1941). The Study of Kinship Systems. *The Journal of the Royal Anthropological Institute of Great Britain and Ireland, 71*(1/2), 1–18.
Renders, A., and Gaeremynck, A. (2012). Corporate governance, principal-principal agency conflicts, and firm value in European listed companies. Corporate Governance: an international review, 20(2), 125–143.
Ritchie, B., & Khorwatt, E. (2007). The attitude of Libyan auditors to inherent control risk assessment. *The British Accounting Review*, 39(1), 39–59.
Rizk, R. (2008) "Islam and Corporate Governance", in Aras, G. and Crowther, D. (eds.), Culture and Corporate Governance Research Series: Issues in Corporate Behaviour and Sustainability, Social Responsibility Network, Leicester, UK, pp. 204–14.
Roe, M. J. (2003). *Political determinants of corporate governance: Political context, corporate impact*. New York: Oxford University Press, Oxford University Press on Demand.
Saidi, N. (2004). Corporate Governance in MENA Countries: Improving Transparency & Disclosure. The Second Middle East and North Africa Regional Corporate Governance Reform. Retrieved from http://www.oecd.org/dataoecd/17/42/33944145.pdf
Samaha, K., Dahawy, K., Hussainey, K., and Stapleton, P. (2012). The extent of corporate governance disclosure and its determinants in a developing market: The case of Egypt. *Advances in Accounting, 28*, 168–178.
Sappington, D. (1991). Incentives in Principal Agent Relationships. *Journal of Economic Perspectives, 3(2)*, 45–66.
Schmoller, G. (1900). *Grundriss der Allgemeinen Volkswirtschaftslehre*. Leipzig: Duncker and Humbolt, Berlin, Germany.
Scott, W. (1995) Institutions and Organisations. Thousand Oaks, CA: Sage Publications.
Scott, W. R. (2001). *Institutions and Organisations*. London: SAGE Publications Inc.
Scott, W. R. (2008). *Institutions and Organisations. Ideas and Interests*. (Third ed). Thousand Oaks, CA: Sage Publications.
Seo, M. G., and Creed, W. D. (2002). Institutional contradictions, praxis, and institutional change: A dialectical perspective. *Academy of Management Review, 27(2)*, 222–247.
Shleifer, A., and Vishny, R. W. (1997). A survey of corporate governance. *The journal of finance*, 52(2), 737–783.
Simon, H. A. (1991). Models of my life. Cambridge, Massachusetts, London, England: MIT press.

Simmons, J. (2004). Managing in the post-managerialist era: Towards socially responsible corporate governance. *Management Decision*, 42(3/4), 601–611.
Solomon, J. (2013). *Corporate governance and accountability*. (Fourth ed). UK: Wiley and Sons Ltd.
Solomon, J., Solomon, A., and Park, C. Y. (2002). A conceptual framework for corporate governance reform in South Korea. *Corporate governance: An international review*, 10(1), 29–46.
Solomon, R. C., and Martin, C. (2004). Above the Bottom Line: An Introduction to Business Ethics (Belmont, CA: Thomson Wadsworth, 3rd edn).
Spencer, H. (1876, 1896, 1910). *The Principles of Sociology* (3 vols). London: Appleton-Century-Crofts.
Sternberg, E. (1997). The defects of stakeholder theory. *Corporate GovernanceAn International Review, 5 (1)*, 3–10.
Stinchcombe, A. (1968). *Constructing Social Theories*. New Yorkrt: Harcourt, Brace and World.
Suddaby, R., and Greenwood, R. (2005). Rhetorical Strategies of Legitimacy. *Administrative Science Quarterly*, *50*(1), 35–67.
Sumner, W. (1906). Folkways. Boston: Ginn and Co.
The US Commercial Service. (2008). *Doing Business in Libya: A Country Commercial Guide for U.S. Companies*. Retrieved from https://s3.amazonaws.com/zanran_storage/www.buyusa.gov/ContentPages/351768.pdf
Thomas, K., and Boolaky, P. (2009). Corporate governance compliance and disclosure in the banking sector: Using data from Japan. Finance and Corporate Governance Conference. Venue: La Trobe University.
Thornton, P. H., and Ocasio, W. (1999). "Institutional logics and the historical contingency of power in organisations: Executive succession in the higher education publishing industry. *American Journal of Sociology, 105(3)*, 801–843.
Thornton, P. H., and Ocasio, W. (2008). Institutional logics,[in:] In Greenwood, R., Oliver, C., Sahlin, K. Suddaby, R. *The SAGE Handbook of Organisational Institutionalism. Sage, London, 99–129.*
Thornton, P. H., Ocasio, W., and Lounsbury, M. (2012). *The institutional logics perspective: A new approach to culture, structure, and process*. Oxford: Oxford University Press, Oxford University Press on Demand.
Tricker, A. (1994). Editorial. *Corporate Governance: An International Review, 2 (1)*, 1–4.
UNCTAD Secretariat. (2006). *Review of the Implementation Status of Corporate Governance Disclosures*, (November), 1–29. UNCTAD United Nations Conference on Trade and Development: Geneva.
UNCTAD. (2011). *Corporate Governance Disclosure in Emerging Markets*. UNCTAD United Nations Conference on Trade and Development: Geneva.
Union of Arab Banks. (2007). *Survey Results: Corporate Governance Survey of the Arab Banking Sector*. Union of Arab Banks. Beirut.
van Gestel, N., and Hillebrand, B. (2011). Explaining Stability and Change: The Rise and Fall of Logics in Pluralistic Fields. *Organisation Studies*, *32*(2), 231–252.
Veblen, T. (1898). Why is economics not an evolutionary science?. *The quarterly journal of economics*, 12(4), 373–397.
Veblen, T. (1919) The Place of Science in Modern Civilization and Other Essays. New York: Huebsch.
Wade, J. B., Porac, J. F., and Pollock, T. G. (1997). Worth, words, and the justi ® cation of executive pay. *Journal of Organisational Behavior*, *18*, 641–664.
Wallace, R. (1987). *Disclosure of Accounting Information in Developing Countries: A Case Study of Nigeria*. Exeter, United Kingdom: (Doctoral Disertation) University of Exeter.
Watson, T. (2007). Organisation theory and HRM. Oxford Handbook of Human Resource Management, The, 108.
Watson, T., and Korczynski, M. (2011). *Sociology, Work and Organisation*. London, United Kingdom: Routledge.

Watts, R. L. (1977). Corporate financial statements, a product of the market and political processes. *Australian Journal of Management, 2*, 53–75.
Weber, M. (1978). *Economy and society: An outline of interpretive sociology* (Vol. 1). Berkeley. Los Angeles. London: Univ of California Press.
Weinberger, O. (1991). *Law, institution and legal politics: fundamental problems of legal theory and social philosophy* (Vol. 14). Dordrecht, the Netherlands: Springer Science and Business Media.
Westphal, J. D., and Zajac, E. J. (1994). Substance and Symbolism in CEOs' Long-Term Incentive Plans. *Administrative Science Quarterly, 39*(3), 367–390.
Westphal, J. D., and Zajac, E. J. (1998). The Symbolic Management of Stockholders: Corporate Governance Reforms and Shareholder Reactions. *Administrative Science Quarterly, 43*(1), 127–153.
Westphal, J. D., and Zajac, E. J. (2001). Decoupling policy from practice: The case of stock repurchase programs. *Administrative Science Quarterly, 46*(2), 202–228.
Williamson, O. E. (1996). The mechanisms of governance. New York: Oxford University Press. Oxford.
Williamson, O. E. (2000). The new institutional economics: taking stock, looking ahead. *Journal of economic literature*, 38(3), 595–613.
Willoughby, W. W. (1896). *An Examination of the Nature of the State: A Study in Political Philosophy*. London, Great Britain: Macmillan.
Wilson, W. (1889). The state and federal governments of the United States: a brief manual for schools and colleges. DC Heath.
Yeung, H. W. C. (2006). Change and continuity in southeast Asian ethnic Chinese business. *Asia Pacific Journal of Management, 23*(3), 229–254. http://doi.org/10.1007/s10490-006-9007-2
Young, M. N., Peng, M. W., Ahlstrom, D., Bruton, G. D., and Jiang, Y. (2008). Corporate governance in emerging economies: A review of the principal–principal perspective. *Journal of management studies*, 45(1), 196–220.
Young, M., and Wilmott, P. (2013). *Family and kinship in East London*. Routledge.
Zagoub, A. A. (2011). *Corporate Governance in Libyan Commercial Banks*. Dundee, Scotland: (Doctoral dissertation) University of Dundee.
Zajac, E. J., & Westphal, J. D. (1995). Accounting for the Explanations of Ceo Compensation - Substance and Symbolism. *Administrative Science Quarterly, 40(2)*, 283–308.
Ziolkowski, R. (2005). *Reexamination of corporate governance concept, Models and Theories and Future Directions*. (doctoral dissertation), University of Canberra. Australia.

List of Figures

https://doi.org/10.1515/9783110602111-008

List of Tables

https://doi.org/10.1515/9783110602111-009

List of Abbreviations

BCSB	The Basel Committee on Banking Supervision
CACG	Commonwealth Association for Corporate Governance
CBL	Central Bank of Libya
CGLSM	Corporate Governance Libyan Stock Market
CGLBS	Corporate Governance of Libyan Banking Sector
CIPE	Centre for International Private Enterprise
EAS	Egypt Accounting Standards
EGX	Egyptian Stock Exchange
NED	Non-Executive Directors
NIE	New Institutional Economics
NIS	New Institutional Sociology (NIS)
NTC	National Transitional Council
GCGF	Global Corporate Governance Forum
MENA	Middle East and North Africa
OECD	Organisation for Economic Co-operation and Development
OIE	Old Institutional Economics
OPEC	Organisation of Petroleum Exporting Countries
IAS	International Accounting Standards
ISAR	International Standards of Accounting and Reporting
LAAA	Libyan Accounting and Auditing Association
LCB	Libyan Commercial Bank
LBS	Libyan banking sector
LSM	Libyan Stock Market
S&P	Standard and Poor
T&D	Transparency and Disclosure
UNCTAD	United Nations Conference on Trade and Development

https://doi.org/10.1515/9783110602111-010

Index

https://doi.org/10.1515/9783110602111-011